THE NEW ASIAN ARCHITECTURE

They were made to write
"In future we will not read backwards. In future we will not read backwards."
A hundred times. Forwards.

– Arundhati Roy, *The God of Small Things*. 1997.

This edition published by
Periplus Editions (HK) Ltd
for sale in Australia, Canada, Indonesia,
Japan, New Zealand and
the United States of America.

Original edition entitled CONTEMPORARY
VERNACULAR: EVOKING TRADITIONS IN
ASIAN ARCHITECTURE published by
Select Books Pte Ltd, Singapore.
Copyright ©1998 Select Books Pte Ltd.

Designed and produced by
Duet Design Pte Ltd

Colour separation by
Superskill Graphics Pte Ltd

Printed in Singapore by
Tien Wah Press

ISBN: 962-593-302-6

THE NEW ASIAN ARCHITECTURE

VERNACULAR TRADITIONS AND CONTEMPORARY STYLE

WILLIAM S.W. LIM

TAN HOCK BENG

PERIPLUS
EDITIONS

VERNACULAR

n. **1**. the. the commonly spoken language or dialect of a particular people or place. **2**. a local style of architecture, in which ordinary houses are built.

CONTENTS

CONTEMPORARY

adj. **1**. living or occurring in the same period. **2**. existing or occurring at the present time. **3**. conforming to modern ideas in style, fashion, etc.

FOREWORD
BY CHARLES CORREA

IF ONE DOES NOT HEAR THE PAST CLEARLY AND HONESTLY, IT CANNOT BECOME PART OF ONE'S WORK. ARCHITECTURE, LIKE THE OTHER VISUAL ARTS, IS IN THE FINAL ANALYSIS THE DOMAIN OF THE INTUITIVE MIND AND EYE.

Implicit in the term "vernacular" is the notion of building as an organic process, involving society as a whole. Those incredibly beautiful houses of the Greek islands, of Rajasthan, of Tahiti – they are not the brainchild of any individual architect, but the product of an entire community, working through its history. For people always seem to have known how to produce the habitat they need, as naturally and intuitively as birds build nests. This is a tradition which exists throughout the world, especially here in Asia.

In contrast to this process, there is of course a more contemporary paradigm, a sort of modern tradition, wherein a piece of architecture is quite clearly the outcome of an individual's idiosyncratic effort. It is a tradition which started with the Renaissance in Europe, and now, by the end of the 20th Century, has spread right across this planet.

Architects in Asia live with both these traditions – as the pioneering examples collected in this book so clearly illustrate. For these societies, industrialisation has not yet closed the doors to the incredibly rich world of the past; on the contrary, that world is very much a part of our everyday lives. Indeed, it is not possible to build in Asia without acknowledging, in one way or another, the presence of the traditional – and the potent ideograms that underlie these traditions. The necessity of understanding this heritage also extends to the construction processes – wherein fine craftsmanship can still be found, and indeed where the distinction between artist and artisan does not exist. (In fact, they both share the same name – *shilpi* – in most Indian languages.)

Most often, of course, these two worlds – the contemporary and the traditional – appear in direct opposition to each other. But this is precisely why Art can be so invaluable – for it can point the way to resolving those differences. This is the real story of the Renaissance – not just that architects and artists learned to be individualistic, but that through this independent stance, they found the freedom to synthesise the opposing mindsets of two totally different cultures which seemed to be on a collision course with each other: the beliefs and practices of the Roman Church and the mythic imagery of ancient Greece and Rome. This is what Michaelangelo, Boromini and the others so brilliantly achieved – through their art, they found a way to bring the rituals of Christianity into the temples of Antiquity.

Such a synthesis is not Janus-faced – i.e. a kind of schizophrenic coexistence of two opposing ideas. On the contrary, it is *one gesture* – which is simultaneously both contemporary and timeless, both "ethnic" and "modern". (In India, handloom cotton fabrics have always been a marvellous example for me of something which is very traditional and yet speaks clearly to our modern sensibilities.) After all, architects are not archaeologists, nor grave diggers. If one does not hear the past clearly and honestly, it cannot become part of one's work. Architecture, like the other visual arts, is in the final analysis the domain of the intuitive mind and eye.

There are two further reasons as to why this book is of such seminal importance. The first concerns the connotations of the word "vernacular". Now to most contemporary architects, this term seems to describe a rather parochial niche (albeit presumably a nostalgic and picturesque one) in an area usually vaguely defined as "Regional Architecture". This, unfortunately, only serves to limit its general interest. In this context, I would submit, that all the great buildings of the past, from Chartres to Fatepur-Sikri, have been regional – in fact, because they so perfectly achieved their goals, they have become (for want of a better word) universal. Then again, those magnificent Oak Park houses of Frank Lloyd Wright are *regional.* They speak of a specific *time* and *place.* They address the particular aspirations that existed among self-made millionaires in Chicago, in the heart of America's Midwest. This is why they communicate so eloquently and passionately to so many architects, living in so many different kinds of places, all around the world.

The second issue also involves a contemporary use of tradition. It underlines even more emphatically the crucial importance of the vernacular – and the compelling reasons for making it accessible to young architects here in Asia. This concerns the shortage of affordable housing in many of our cities, a subject which must surely be at the top of the agenda for most Asian governments. Here we must reiterate the fact that through the centuries, every society has succeeded in building shelters perfectly in consonance with its needs and resources. There is hardly any need or scope for "improvement" in the various vernacular languages of housing generated indigenously around the world – just as there is absolutely no need to tinker with the typologies of, say, Georgian terrace houses in London (which, in the context of this essay, can be perceived to be a form of indigenous vernacular). In fact, if you examine all the virtues so dear to the hearts of environmentalists today – e.g. the recycling of materials, balanced ecosystems, and so forth – you will find that incredibly inventive solutions already exist. In fact, have *existed for centuries.*

What no longer exists, of course, is the modern urban context in which these marvellous solutions are viable. This then is our task: to ensure that our cities, in the course of their rapid growth, adopt planning codes and densities that are able to accept these indigenous patterns of vernacular habitat. This will have decisive implications on the amount of investment needed to address the shortfall of affordable housing, the numbers and types of jobs generated, and so forth – for it will bring back into the process of construction a whole lot of players who otherwise are rapidly becoming disenfranchised.

And to this task of modifying the urban context, the architect must bring his professional skills, i.e. his visual and topological skills, and not just a generalised sense of compassion – like Florence Nightingale moving among the wounded. What we *do not* have to do is design mass housing for people. On the contrary, the wonderfully flexible and pluralistic language of vernacular habitat already exists. All we must do, as architects and planners, is adjust our cities so that this language becomes viable again. And once this is accomplished, then our remaining task will be to just get out of the way.

August 1997

PREFACE

"In reality design is itself an instrument of research into the problem posed and not simply a search for a solution."

– Pierre von Meiss, *Elements of Architecture: From Form to Place*, 1989.

In the face of globalisation and the transcending power of the media, the role of architecture in place-making and in the evocation of specific traditions has been questioned. Many architects are producing works that are merely "free-floating signs", or what critic Michael Hays termed "... purely abstract, technical signifiers without context which, volatilized by our postmodern perceptual apparatuses (accustomed as they are to channel flipping and image sampling), now flow like vapour into what critics call the 'hyperspace' that consumer capital has constructed for itself". [1]

Yet, despite the perceived homogenisation, the assertion of cultural specificity is in no way less vigorous. Manuel Castells suggests that against the normative trend of a computer networked world, "local societies, territorially defined, must preserve their identities, and build on their historical roots, regardless of their economic and functional dependence upon the space of flows". [2]

In the context of Asia, it has become quite apparent that conscientious architects have been pursuing an engagement with traditions and the specifics of locality with renewed vigour during the last couple of decades. The impetus for this book was the recognition of this increasing consciousness. In June 1996 AA Asia, which comprises a group of Asian architects that shares and debates ideas on a regular basis, held a two-day workshop in Singapore entitled "Contemporary Vernacular". The ideas presented were to become the embryonic framework for this book. A subsequent international conference, scheduled to take place in Beijing in September 1997, served to act as an invigorating catalyst, and provided the stimulus for a greater elaboration and continuation of the book's main thrust.

All the architects featured in the book are concerned with the understanding of a specific architecture that engages with its temporal and geographical context. This is extremely difficult for architects working in a new global milieu, where the definition of individual and collective identity has become highly complex. Notions of identity have always been intricately related to traditions. It is ironic that the term "tradition" usually carries with it connotations of backwardness – of being limited by history and precedents.

Yet many architects are now decrying the loss of a sense of place. The works featured are the tangible manifestations of such impulses. They are not easily categorised, and the attempt at grouping them in the book is merely to present the various issues and formal manifestations within an essentially larger framework of concerns. Hopefully, the process of articulating such a general categorisation will reveal the complex dimensions involved.

On one side stand some architects self-consciously promoting the use of traditional imagery in their search for new answers. Their works attempt to embrace meanings which have become embedded in the cultural tradition. Although they are essentially using a language of prefabricated meanings, they are clearly distinguished from the regressive return to the forms of the past – the pastiche, or symbolic "hats" placed atop utilitarian blocks – through their refined sense of craftsmanship and tectonic presence. Their works are not merely architectural signs tacked onto perfunctory containers. They differ from Robert Venturi's "decorated shed" in the way they handle and use traditional modes of construction.

On the other side stand a number of architects keen to combine previous iconography with their own highly personal aesthetics and idiosyncrasies. Some have found it more meaningful to conduct a search to extend the presence of traditions in a more abstract manner. Still others have attempted to evolve a modernist idiom that only hints at past models. Convincing syntheses of the best of tradition and scientific modernism are rare. However, many of these architects have produced an interesting body of works that are difficult to ignore. They are intense and carry with them their own regenerative force and a certain vitality.

This wide range of alternative strategies and variations should not be seen merely at the formal level. The lessons present in these projects go beyond "scenographic picturesqueness". Their forthrightness of approach and a committed engagement with the issue of tradition will surely be redefined and become more wide-ranging in response. It is a growing process of exploration, evaluation and validation – one that suggests an even wider range of future approaches and possibilities. Pierre von Meiss argues that "in reality design is itself an instrument of research into the problem posed and not simply a search for a solution."[3] Hopefully, new paradigms will be forged.

1. Michael Hays, 1993. "Frank Gehry and the Vitra Design Museum" in *GSD NEWS*, Harvard Graduate School of Design.
2. Castells, Manuel, 1993. *The Informational City*, Oxford, UK and Cambridge, USA: Blackwell, p. 350.
3. Pierre von Meiss, 1989. *Elements of Architecture: From Form to Place.* London: Van Nostrand Reinhold (International).

CHAPTER 1

THE FUTURE OF ASIA'S PAST

In the past few decades, countries in East and Southeast Asia have adopted the free market economy in order to maximise the benefits of private initiative. This has generated enormous energy and has sustained the necessary dynamism for continuous changes and economic development. Many of these countries, particularly the four newly industrialised economies (NIEs) namely Hong Kong, Singapore, South Korea and Taiwan, have undergone unprecedented economic growth and social transformation. In the early '80s, three Asean countries, i.e. Thailand, Malaysia and Indonesia, with much larger populations and greater natural resources than the other Asean countries, quickly learned and effectively adopted many of the development strategies already in use in the fully industrialised nations of the world. They too have succeeded in achieving continuous rapid economic growth. Under the leadership of Deng Xiaoping (whose policies, since his recent demise, are closely adhered to by his successor), China follows close behind.

Rapid urbanisation continues, particularly in the primate cities. At present, China is experiencing an incredible magnitude of urban migration which has been projected to exceed 100 million by the year 2000 AD. Rapid economic development and job availability are the major "*pull*" factors causing the migration. The strain on existing infrastructure and social services are becoming increasingly apparent. In contrast, the rapid urbanisation in slow-growth developing economies is caused by the "*push*" factor of over-population, joblessness and poverty

THE ENERGY GENERATED BY THE FREE MARKET ECONOMY, WORKING IN TANDEM WITH THE POSITIVE ROLE PLAYED BY GOVERNMENTS AND INDIVIDUAL ENTREPRENEURS, IS NOW WIDELY ACCEPTED AS THE MAGIC FORMULA FOR RAPID ECONOMIC DEVELOPMENT.

in the rural areas. This has inevitably resulted in the spread of squatter settlements and shanty towns as well as in an increase in crimes, unemployment and lawlessness.

The energy generated by the free market economy, working in tandem with the positive role played by governments and individual entrepreneurs, is now widely accepted as the magic formula for rapid economic development. This is reflected in the new wealth of the successful business and professional classes and the rapid growth of the relatively affluent middle-income group.[1]

In Europe the industrial revolution with its accompanying technological inventions provided the necessary basis for establishing an intellectual and aesthetic revolution. Bauhaus was established during the inter-war years, and carried out exciting and wide-ranging experiments in the arts as well as in architecture. In the meantime, progressive architects formulated the Declaration of Athens Charter, with which a new architecture was born and Modernism was firmly established. With great confidence, Le Corbusier and his contemporaries wrote, lectured, planned and built, to establish a brave new world based on the advancement of modern science and technology.

After World War Two, the USA dominated the non-communist world and American corporations and multinationals progressively expanded their territorial influence. With this shift in power, the vision of architecture and urbanism was progressively distorted by corporate professional practices and commercialism, which have resulted in the simplification and deculturalisation of Modernism into what is now known as the "International Style" – a post-War aesthetic tool of American Capitalism. This approach to architectural design ignores the environmental context, is disinterested in climatic conditions, and has no cultural references. The International Style has lost much of the original dynamism of Modernism.

Since the late 'sixties, many urbanists have seriously questioned the existing western urban development model. These urbanists include Jane Jacob who lamented the sterility of American cities, Robert Venturi who celebrated the complexity of Las Vegas, and the author's criticism of the inequitable distribution of economic benefits.[2] Furthermore, its architectural expressions and planning theories have since been humbled and debunked by the onslaught of an Existentialism-inspired value revolution and its subsequent post-Modernism.

For the past two to three decades, western architects and architectural critics have visited and studied the city of Tokyo. They have been, and continue to be, fascinated, disturbed and surprised. The Japanese have broken much of the accepted planning rules in creating Tokyo, yet the city's dynamism remains and has even developed over time. Tokyo is full of excitement and surprises. In its apparent chaos, there is order – an order, seemingly, of irrationality.

In 1990, Venturi and Scott Brown visited Tokyo. These "two naifs" were amazed and delighted with their dis-

IT IS THUS
UNDERSTANDABLE
THAT CITIFS ARE
NOW OFTEN PLANNED,
BUILT, AND
EXPANDED, EITHER
ON THE BASIS OF
HALF-HEARIED
APPLICATIONS OF
OUTDATED PLANNING
THEORIES, OR ON
NOTHING MORE THAN
ECONOMIC CRITERIA
AND MARKET FORCES.

coveries: "Tokyo has its act together – though granted it is a chaotic act. ... But is not this a convincing chaos or an order that is not yet understood *by the West* – (the italics are the author's) or an ambiguity without anguish?"[3]

More recently, urbanists have been struggling to understand the impact of rapid technological development and pluralism on cultural values and lifestyles. In his book *S.M.L.XL.*, Rem Koolhaas has introduced a new dimension to urbanism by clearly defining the importance of scale and size.[4] However, the recent discovery by western urbanites of the complexity and contradiction of Asian cities has further enforced this author's belief in the ignorance and misconception about Asia and its cultural environment which is prevalent among westerners.

Like Tokyo, most Asian cities have paid only lip-service to the numerous foreign advisors and experts who have proffered their recommendations on architectural design and city planning. Thus, cities such as Hong Kong and Bangkok have developed their own character, and each can offer the interested observer different but equally exciting experiences.

However, the authorities in most Asian cities do not have the will, the financial resources or the management capabilities to effectively improve the urban infrastructure and to confront, for example, the traffic gridlock in Bangkok, the degradation of the urban poor and extensive squatter settlements in Manila as well as the excessive pollution and increasing traffic paralysis in many major Asian urban centres.

It has taken a long time for planners to realise that cities are extremely complex organisms. Like the eco-system in nature, they are very sensitive and responsive to outside intervention. However, to date there is no alternative model, which is capable of accomplishment, available. It is thus understandable that cities are now often planned, built, and expanded, either on the basis of half-hearted applications of outdated planning theories, or on nothing more than economic criteria and market forces.

Singapore is the only Asian city which has strictly planned and implemented its various "Master Plans" on the ideological basis of western planning theories. These include the use of zoning, height and plot-ratio control, and the building hierarchy from "downtown" – the original, main city centre – to new towns and neighbourhood centres. Singapore's efficient transport system and clean-green image have deservedly won international acclaim. However, the city is over-regulated. It lacks excitement and surprises, as well as the delightfully unexpected – or even unintended.

Today, cross-cultural exchanges become increasingly meaningful and mutually beneficial. Creative arts and great ideas from anywhere in the world can be understood and appreciated across cultural frontiers. With the availability of the mass media, these arts and ideas can be transmitted quickly and convincingly. New values and lifestyles are evolving at an ever rapid pace. These can be creative, artistic and enlightened, or offensive, decadent and trivial. The contemporary world culture generates

THIS ALL-EMBRACING
CONTEMPORARY
WORLD CULTURE
AND THE
RELATIONSHIP
BETWEEN TRADITION
AND MODERNITY
MUST BE BETTER
UNDERSTOOD.

exciting new possibilities, but sometimes the possibilities bring disturbing consequences.

With the rapid introduction of computers, the Internet and other sophisticated forms of computerised media, the contemporary world culture is both affecting and supported by an increasingly large segment of the world population across national and ethnic boundaries. This new culture has great appeal. Pluralism and rebelliousness as well as tolerance and freedom are its essential ingredients. These trends add richness to our lives and our visual environment. New solutions are continuously being introduced in response to our new lifestyles and expectations. In the 21st Century, we will need to re-examine the nature and locations of work places as well as their larger implications in relation to the changing functions of the city itself.

This all-embracing contemporary world culture and the relationship between tradition and modernity must be better understood. In Asia, we have often incorrectly identified this contemporary culture as "western culture", since it is usually associated with Coca-Cola, McDonald's and blue jeans, as well as with new and changing lifestyles. In fact, however, this contemporary culture belongs to everyone, to all of us who live in today's world. This contemporary culture evolves continuously, with input from everywhere around the globe. Let's ask ourselves this question: is a pop singer or an installation artist from Japan or Indonesia any *less* contemporary than one from Europe or the United States?

In recent years, there have been an increasing number of confrontational debates and critical comments relating to the conflict of cultures between the East and the West. These debates, which are being conducted with increasing intensity, involve respectable western scholars. Notwithstanding the fact that their analyses have been seriously challenged by many scholars from both Asia and the West. Asians should take their observations seriously.

It should be noted, however, that the conflict between the cultures is *not* about the past. Rather, the conflict is about the differences in perception of today's contemporary world culture. Historically, in particular in relation to rapidly changing values and lifestyles, it was the West that generated the early development of ideas and energies. It is therefore understandable that many in the West still have a strong proprietary sense to them. Furthermore, today the assertive East is increasingly vocal in challenging the need to accept what it perceives as negative aspects of contemporary world culture. In this process of dissent, serious efforts are being made to formulate effective methods of intervention based on traditional Eastern cultures, values and lifestyles.

The Prime Minister of Singapore, Mr Goh Chok Tong, has suggested the need to develop a set of shared values which Singaporeans of all races and faiths can subscribe to and live by. To quote from a recent government publication entitled *Shared Values*:

The four core values are "*placing society above self, upholding the family as the basic building block of society,*

THE POSITIVE
ASPECTS OF OUR
TRADITIONAL VALUES
WILL HAVE TO BE
RECOGNISED AND
SUPPORTED BEFORE
THEY CAN BE
ADOPTED,
TRANSFORMED AND
INTEGRATED INTO
OUR FAST-EVOLVING
VALUE SYSTEM.

resolving major issues through consensus instead of conten-
tion, and stressing racial and religious tolerance and har-
mony."[5]

Perhaps we should also accept the possibility that
"the relative importance and character of civil society in
East and Southeast Asia differ fundamentally from the
historical experiences of earlier industrialising capitalist
societies."[6]

Many countries in the region which are now experiencing a high economic growth will encounter an unprecedented rate of urbanisation. In the inevitable process of
urban redevelopment, which is likely to be based on existing planning theories, much of the old historical areas
will be destroyed. With great haste, thousands of inap-
propriate and ineptly designed buildings will be constructed. Where it has not already happened, it will be
a case of the free market gone mad. There is no time to
think or reflect. The bottom line is economic viability,
and the driving force is financial greed. In many urban
centres of the emerging Asian economies a pseudo-
stylistic historicism is fast gaining popular acceptance,
particularly for the newly rich. The buildings designed
under this impetus provide their new owners with an
"attractive" alternative to what they perceive as the bor-
ing and monotonous International Style. However, these
pseudo-stylistic historic buildings are not only devoid of
design principles, they are usually aesthetically offensive.
They are buildings built because they can be produced
fast, with the minimum of professional effort.

Our own heritage needs to be effectively understood
and integrated into our evolving value system. This is necessary in order to provide a distinct identity for the
community. At the same time, we must examine the differences and commonalities of the traditional values of
different cultures, and the increasing convergence of values and lifestyles arising from the common acceptance of
today's contemporary world culture. Can our traditional
cultures and heritages be preserved? Even if they are,
are they relevant any longer? Traditional values can either
provide strength and identity or be obstructive to the
development process and the acceptance of today's more
enlightened values. The positive aspects of our traditional
values will have to be recognised and supported before
they can be adopted, transformed and integrated into our
fast-evolving value system.[7] This process is very complex,
especially in relation to the development of the arts
and architecture. Official patronage – as illustrated by
the support given by Prince Charles to historic revi-
valism in the United Kingdom today – can be potentially
disastrous.

It is in this context that we have identified the phe-
nomenon – practised by many leading Asian architects –
of modernising the vernacular. It is interesting to note
that many of these architects have developed their own
interpretations in relative isolation; it is only in recent
years that these architects have begun to have a notice-
able influence on each other. The successful use of the
vernacular has been applied to a wide range of building

types. These include houses and resort hotels as well as museums, institutional and educational buildings. However, the term "vernacular idiom" does not mean nostalgia – such as depicted by the Grand Hotel in Taipei – nor an exercise in replication, such as seen in the extension of the Raffles Hotel in Singapore. If applied incorrectly, the results of the vernacular idiom can be disastrous.

Where will this contemporary use of the vernacular lead us? Is it a myth – a passing phase and a temporary phenomenon, artificially created? At this point it is important to realise that the essence of Modernism and its subsequent philosophical and aesthetic development have often not been understood by many architects in Asian countries. At the same time, a respect for tradition and our own architectural heritage is widely acceptable. They provide the basic foundations towards developing an exciting contemporary reinterpretation of the vernacular.

In this pluralistic world, architects are continually confronted with new design directions. Perhaps this is a new architectural direction of post-Modernism, as this design approach can be more easily developed and adapted by the emerging Asian economies. In the process, the future of our past will be assured and recognised. If nothing else is achieved, the cities of Asia can at least avoid many unwanted atrocities – atrocities which are the result of a misunderstood Modernism – during the transitional stage of economic development in the initial decades of the new millennium.

1. Richard Robinson and David S.G. Goodman, eds. 1996. *The New Rich in Asia: Mobile Phones, McDonald's and the Middle Class Revolution*. London: Routledge.
2. William S.W. Lim. 1975. *Equity and urban environment in the third world*, Singapore: DP Consultant Service Pte Ltd.
3. Robert Venturi and Denise Scott Brown. 1991. *Architecture and Decorative Arts*, Japan: Kajima Institute Publishing Co. Ltd.
4. Rem Koolhaas and Bruce Mau. 1995. *S,M,L,XL*. Rotterdam: 010 Publishers.
5. Singapore Cmd 1 of 1991. *Shared Values*. Presented to Parliament by Command of the President of the Republic of Singapore: 2 January 1991.
6. Michael R.J. Vatiliotis. 1996. *Political Change in Southeast Asia; Trimming the Banyan Tree*. London: Routledge.
7. William S.W. Lim. 1993. "Contemporary Culture + Heritage = Localism". Paper presented at the *International Conference on Architecture, (Post) Modernity and Difference*, Organised by the School of Architecture, National University of Singapore, Singapore. April 1993. Published in *Solidarity*, No. 139/140, July – December 1993.

CHAPTER 2

MODERNISING APPROPRIATIONS/ APPROPRIATING MODERNITY

Traditional architecture is a result of man's elemental needs and his intricate relationships with the society and the environment he lives in. In an era when the real world appears to sublimate into cyberspace, an explicit desire for a return to the past is perhaps understandable.

Critic Kenneth Frampton, who is responsible for popularising the term "Critical Regionalism", advocates that universal civilisation – which he refers to as a civilisation of capitalism – is opposed to regional culture. He sees regionalism as the answer to French historian Paul Ricoeur's quest of "how to become modern and to return to the sources". Ricoeur has posed the question:

"In order to get on to the road toward modernisation, is it necessary to jettison the old cultural past which has been the raison d'etre *of a nation? ... It is a fact: every culture cannot sustain and absorb the shock of modern civilisation. There is the paradox: how to become modern and to return to the sources ..."*

Frampton sees regionalism as a strategy of resistance:

"Everything will depend on the capacity of rooted culture to recreate its own tradition while appropriating foreign influences at the level of both culture and civilisation ... Regionalism is a dialectical expression. It self-consciously seeks to deconstruct universal Modernism, in terms of values and images which are quintessentially rooted, and at the same time to adulterate these basic references with paradigms drawn from alien sources... Any attempt to circumvent this dialectical synthesis through a recourse to superficial historicism can only result in consumerist iconography

masquerading as culture." [1]

Frampton further postulates that the future trend in architecture will be moulded in the Pacific Basin region. Others have heralded the birth of a new cultural ecology, that of the Pacific Rim. These visions of an architectural Pacific Century and the euphoria generated by the anticipation of a trade-driven "Pacific Age" coincide with forecasts in other disciplines such as business, economics, industry and tourism, which have predicted that the Age of the North Atlantic will yield in the 21st Century to that of the Pacific.

Hence, attention is gradually being focused on the development of the interacting cultures of these societies in transition, and the relationship of such interaction to traditional buildings. It is crucial to examine how these significant indigenous archetypes – that have developed over such a long period of time – can be reinterpreted and applied to modern living.

Today, issues concerning the growing ecological consciousness as well as the ideological quest for national roots are extensively debated, and inherent prejudices are examined dispassionately. Regionalism is seen as a counter-trend to the universalising force of modern architecture, and as a manifestation of identity. In Southeast Asia, quite a number of architects of opposing persuasions have felt the urgent and irrepressible need for previously neglected cultural introspection and for the formulation of national or even regional identities in design.

But this quest is often associated with a sentimental

THE CRITICAL ASPECT
OF ALL DEFINITIONS
OF TRADITION
IMPLIES THAT IT IS
SOMETHING HANDED
DOWN OR
TRANSMITTED FROM
ONE GENERATION TO
THE NEXT.

approach to the regionalism of the past, with its emphasis on contextual reference and ethnicity. Often, this has developed into an architecture of nostalgia – one that is revivalist, scenographic and ethnocentric. An exploitative form in which regionalism resurfaces in the 20th Century is tourism, in which an architecture of tourist commercialism based on a familiarization with the past is produced. Architects are turning to vernacular architecture as sources for inspiration.

The term "vernacular architecture" is one of the most commonly used but least understood terms in the region. Vernacular structures, which are in essence "architecture without architects", provide many basic lessons for architects. These time-proven indigenous shelters were invariably built by anonymous local craftsmen who used local techniques and materials. These indigenous dwellings are well adapted to the extremes of climate and their particular environmental setting. Such dwellings reflect their society's accumulated wisdom and collective images. They are imbued with cosmological and religious values, social and political structures, sensibility and attitude towards time and space. Their forms and proportions, craftsmanship and decorations, are symbolic and meaningful. They do not have aesthetic pretensions, hence their generating principles are devoid of any straining after originality.

In vernacular settlements, the architectural language is deeply embedded as an aspect of tradition. Such tradition assures the continuity of vernacular settings through codified imagery, materials and technology. Forms and symbolism are empirically known and stable, while change occurs in an incremental manner.

The term "tradition" comes from the Latin verb *trado-transdo*, meaning "to pass on to another". Tradition is elusive and difficult to define in a wholly satisfactory way, although various attempts have been made. Edward Shils sees it as "*... anything which is transmitted or handed down from the past to the present. It makes no statement about what is handed down or in what particular combination, or whether it is a physical object or a cultural construction; it says nothing about how long it has been handed down or in what manner, whether orally or in written form.*"[2]

The critical aspect of all definitions of tradition implies that it is something handed down or transmitted from one generation to the next. Implicit in this notion is the double process of preserving and transmitting. Curtis argues that "*Tradition in the obvious sense of a visible past inheritance can only be partly helpful, for reality today is different. The architect must find what is right for the present circumstances and if he is sufficiently probing and profound he will make a valid addition to the stock of forms. There is no place for passeisme or for a bogus, revivalist sentimentality.*"[3]

The terms "traditional" and "vernacular" have also been used interchangeably because tradition is synechdochic for vernacular. This is because the qualities that we associate with tradition are also found in the vernacular.[4] Dell Upton has argued that the approaches of scholars of traditional environments from the so-called First and

**THE POSITING OF
A DICHOTOMY
BETWEEN NON-
WESTERN AND
WESTERN DIVIDES
THE WORLD INTO
DIAMETRICALLY
OPPOSING
COMPARTMENTS.**

Third Worlds suffer from comparable limitations. Both groups work on theories of tradition and the vernacular – which are static and dualistic in their conception – that came from European intellectual history. Both are also "grounded in an elusive faith in the object as authentic sign of its maker."[5]

These concepts of a distinctive social-cultural space termed "traditional" or "vernacular" arose in the 17th and 18th Centuries in Europe, where the "picturesque exoticism" was the motivating factor in the study of traditional architecture. This acknowledgment of difference not only promoted a circumstantial view of history, it also reinforced the dualistic views of *us* and *them*. The positing of a dichotomy between non-Western and Western divides the world into diametrically opposing compartments.

This dichotomy in thinking which views things as "outside" and "inside" includes an implicit opposition – that between stability and change. The vernacular is widely seen as stable, representing enduring values, and therefore authentic. The opposition is between active and passive building traditions. The vernacular is thus seen as traditional. Bernard Rudofsky argues that *"Vernacular architecture does not go through fashion cycles. It is nearly immutable, indeed, unimprovable, since it serves its purpose to perfection. As a rule, the origin of indigenous building forms and construction methods is lost in the past."*[6]

Upton sees Rudofsky's view as symptomatic of the duality that sets the vernacular aside as a distinct category of experience with a negative aspect. Seen as stable and passive, it is perceived as stagnant, and hence marginalised in the changing world that characterises the human landscape.

Current studies of vernacular landscapes and architecture tend to stress continuity and authenticity. Upton suggests that *"we need to contaminate the space of the vernacular and to relocate it in the human cultural landscape. We should turn our attention away from a search for the authentic, the characteristic, the enduring and the pure, and immerse ourselves in the active, the evanescent and the impure, seeking settings that are ambiguous, multiple, often contested, and examining points of contact and transformation – in the market, at the edge, in the new and the decaying."*[7]

This indicates a need to venture beyond insular and exclusive tendencies towards a more global and inclusive architecture. Jennifer Wicke argues that *"Regionalism also fantasises a local conversation, a regional 'essence' that, however desirable in utopian terms, cannot be located anywhere on the map of postmodern reality. The preservationist and idiomatic references that have arisen out of critical regionalism are all to the good, but a complete regionalist program founders on the politics of the global, which cannot be waved away by the magic wand of a regionally sensitive architecture. The social space, after all, is at least as much constituted by the informational, representational networks of mass culture and media as by anything else, and a regional purism will throw out the baby of social reality with the bath water of internationalism."*[8]

ONLY IF WE
RECOGNISE OUR
TRADITION AS A
HERITAGE THAT IS
CONTINUALLY
EVOLVING WILL WE
BE ABLE TO FIND THE
CORRECT BALANCE
BETWEEN REGIONAL
AND INTERNATIONAL
IDENTITIES.

The notion of a contemporary vernacular can thus be defined as a self-conscious commitment to uncover a particular tradition's unique responses to place and climate, and thereafter to exteriorise these formal and symbolic identities into creative new forms through an artist's eye that is very much in touch with contemporary realities and lasting human values. Many scholars have rejected the definition of tradition as a set of fixed attributes, and architects in Asia have attempted to define tradition in new ways.

Only if we recognise our tradition as a heritage that is continually evolving will we be able to find the correct balance between regional and international identities. The architect needs to decide which past principles are still appropriate and valid for today's reality, and how best to incorporate these with modern building requirements and current constructional methods. The aim is at innovation rather than duplication.

The response to this context is crucial. A temporal equation is forced upon every architectural decision. What of the old should one retain, and what reject? These issues are extremely pertinent and merit serious debate. Instead of viewing tradition and modernity as mutually exclusive polar opposites, one should regard them as complementary in nature.

One is reminded of T.S. Eliot's theory of the relationship between tradition and novelty in his famous essay of 1919, "Tradition and the Individual Talent". Although Eliot's elucidation of the structure of relationships be-

tween quotation and invention referred to literature, and to poetry in particular, architecture shares a similar relationship. According to Eliot, a true sense of tradition is a sense of the timeless and the temporal together.

Eliot suggests that *"Tradition ... cannot be inherited, and if you want it you must obtain it by great labour. It involves in the first place, a historical sense, which ... involves a perception, not only of the pastness of the past, but of its presence ... The past should be altered by the present as much as the present is directed by the past ... the difference between the present and the past is that the conscious present is an awareness of the past in a way and to an extent which the past's awareness of itself cannot show."*

A number of recent projects in Asia have been strikingly successful in this respect. Examples of significant regionalist works in different parts of the world demostrate a high level of collaboration between the architects and the indigenous craftsman. In Asia, this pool of skilled craftsmen is still relatively large. Hence, each of these architects is pursuing his own path, emanating from his personal philosophy and architectural temperament and sensibility – yet each is consciously urging, through his or her work, a genuine espousing of knowledge of the social as well as a conscious respect for the indigenous culture.

These works demonstrate several ways of dealing with the vernacular and the notion of tradition. Shils argues that *"constellations of symbols, clusters of images, are received and modified. They change in the process of trans-*

TRADITION IS THUS
LIKELY TO UNDERGO
CHANGES IN THE
PROCESS OF
TRANSMISSION AND
ACTS OF POSSESSION,
ALTHOUGH IMPORTANT
ELEMENTS REMAIN
DISCERNIBLE.

mission as interpretations are made of the tradition presented; they change also while they are in the possession of their recipients. This chain of transmitted variants of a tradition is also called a tradition, as in the 'Platonic tradition' or the 'Kantian tradition'."[9]

Tradition is thus likely to undergo changes in the process of transmission and acts of possession, although important elements remain discernible. The rejection of the imagistic use of symbols does not imply a rejection of tradition. Architecture contributes to tradition in the process of continual transformation. T.S. Eliot's verses may be elucidating here :

What we call the beginning is often the end
And to make an end is to make a beginning .
The end is where we start from. And every phrase
And sentence that is right (where every word is at home
Taking its place to support the others,
The work neither diffident nor ostentatious,
An easy commerce of the old and the new,
The common word exact without vulgarity,
The formal word precise but not pedantic,
The complete consort dancing together)
Every phrase and every sentence is an end
and a beginning ... [10]

1. Kenneth Frampton, 1982. "Modern Architecture and the Critical Present", *Architectural Design Profile*, 52:7-8, p.77.
2. Edward Shils. *Tradition*, USA: The University of Chicago Press, p.12.
3. William Curtis, 1989. "On Creativity, Imagination and the Design Process" in *Space For Freedom: The Search for Architectural Excellence in Muslim Societies*, Ismail Serageldin, London: Butterworth Architecture, p. 234
4. Dell Upton, 1993. "The Tradition of Change" in *Traditional Dwellings and Settlements Review*, Vol. V(1), pp. 9-165.
5. Ibid, p. 10.
6. Bernard Rudofsky, 1964. *Architecture Without Architects: A Short Introduction to Non-Pedigreed Architecture*, New York: Doubleday.
7. D. Upton, p. 14.
8. Jennifer Wicke, 1993. "Building a Practice: Scogin Elam and Bray and Social Space" in Mark Linder, ed., *Scogin Elam and Bray : Critical Architecture/Architectural Criticism*, New York: Rizzoli.
9. Ibid, p. 13.
10. T.S. Eliot, 1944. "Little Gidding", *Four Quartets*, London: Faber & Faber.

CHAPTER 3

CONTEMPORARY VERNACULAR OF EMERGING ECONOMIES IN ASIA

The development of a culture of modernity on a community is a slow process. For the individual, it can be painful and disrupting. It can also be exciting and liberating. Many existing values will be questioned and discarded, while others will be transmuted and modified. In many instances, this takes two to three generations, as experienced by many rural folk moving to large urban centres and by migrants in a new land and an unfamiliar cultural environment. Old values, customs, cultures and lifestyles continue through strong family ties.

Since the end of the World War Two, we have been experiencing an ever-increasing pace of what David Harvey called "time-space compression".[1] To avoid becoming an intellectual dinosaur in an increasingly pluralistic and complex contemporary society, we need within a working life-span to up-grade as well as to learn and unlearn continuously in response to the rapid changes in values, life styles and technological innovations. However, this challenging process has yet to be widely accepted, even in the developed economies.

During the last three decades, the rate of economic growth and urban development in the emerging economies of East and Southeast Asia has been unprecedented, and has generated major social, cultural and environmental upheavals. Traditional urban areas have been destroyed and the surrounding agricultural land absorbed.

Singapore's unique experience is both admirable and disturbing. Singapore has effectively applied the theoretical planning models of the pioneers in the modern move-

THE MAIN DRIVING
FORCE OF THE RECENT
RAPID ECONOMIC
DEVELOPMENT IS THE
ACCEPTANCE OF A
POWERFUL AND
UNCOMPROMISING
IDEOLOGY OF PROFIT-
DRIVEN CAPITALISM.

ment. The city functions well. It is clean and green. How-ever, it is very expensive to maintain, besides also being predictable and unexciting. Rem Koolhaas, the imminent urban theorist, recently described Singapore's physical transformation thus : "... the city represents the ideologi-cal production of the past three decades in its pure form, uncontaminated by surviving contextual remnants".[2]

However, in most cities in the Asean emerging econo-mies, the changes have been less regulated and controlled. Reflecting the incredible rate of economic development, the recent drastic physical changes of China's coastal cities is unimaginable. Within a decade, much of the traditional areas are rapidly being demolished and new constructions, including many high rise buildings, are multitudinous.

The development of modernity in many Asian coun-tries is disrupted and distorted by wars and ideologically-based social experiments, as well as by corrupt and incompetent governments. The main driving force of the recent rapid economic development is the acceptance of a powerful and uncompromising ideology of profit-driven capitalism. Fortunately, most Asian countries introduced substantial modifications to their development strategies before implementation to suit local conditions, and have therefore avoided the unpleasant consequences being faced by Russia today.

Emerging economies in the Asian region, such as China and Vietnam, have very little knowledge of the history and development which has led to Modernism and Post-Modernism. The intellectual energy and discourse under-lying Modernism and Post-Modernism and their subse-quent aesthetic development are seldom understood or appreciated. It is therefore not surprising that thousands of high-rise buildings are being constructed in the region with a total disregard to basic design principles. Driven by free market forces, there is no time to think, learn or reflect. The bottom line is economic viability and the driving force is a greed for money. The standard of taste is appalling. Recognition is given to competence, efficiency and speed. Design quality and innovative ideas are sel-dom heeded or even acknowledged.

The political and business elite find that replication, i.e. copying and modifying, are generally acceptable. However, when replication is done too frequently and too indis-criminately, the historical importance of the original pro-duct loses its true meaning and significance. Fortunately, "grandeur replication", i.e. larger-than-life reproduction of traditional forms and images as an aesthetic expres-sion, is now used less frequently and is seldom applied to large urban projects. However, notwithstanding their in-tellectual pretensions, these aesthetic solutions do pro-vide a much needed response and perhaps a temporary satisfaction to counter rapid value changes, cultural un-certainty and aesthetic confusion.

It is in this context that we have identified the phe-nomenon of the contemporary use of the vernacular by many leading Asian architects. The extensive use of local materials and craftsmanship and the application of

CONTEMPORARY
VERNACULAR CAN
THEREFORE BE
CONSIDERED AS A
DYNAMIC
DEVELOPMENT OF
ARCHITECTURAL
DIRECTION TO MEET
THE CHALLENGES OF
RAPID URBANISATION
AND DEVELOPMENT IN
THE ASIAN EMERGING
ECONOMIES.

appropriate technology together with the introduction of contemporary approaches to plan arrangements, spatial relationships and visual complexity have provided the basis in modernising traditions. As the essence of traditional architecture is generally understood, this design approach should be more easily acceptable by both the teachers and students of architecture in the emerging economies. Its strong identification with local conditions is more meaningful and should provide a positive response in generating innovative and visually exciting solutions.

The continuous self-inventing intellectualisation of aesthetic theories of the metropolis appears to have exhausted itself at present with the increasing global culture. The question of whether a contemporary vernacular will soon be accepted into the mainstream architectural direction is uncertain. Not long ago, a leading Asian metropolitan convert commented: "Charles Correa is great, but he is so provincial!" More recently, a western critic's remark on seeing Geoffrey Bawa's exhibition, as "[it is] very exciting, but what is the fuss about?" is also rather telling. Fortunately, the metropolitan dominance of architectural and design directions cannot now be sustained for much longer, as the provinces have already posed serious challenges for a rightful and deserving place in this increasingly complex and pluralistic world.

Perhaps the recent emergence of many Asian economies has encouraged the re-surfacing of long submerged and sometimes discredited values of various traditional societies. Notwithstanding their diverse interpretations, the buzz word is "Asian Values". Without going through the vigorous exercise of adaptation and transmutation, this has often resulted in serious conflicts with and diverging views from the rapidly changing and dominant global cultural values and lifestyles.

Contemporary vernacular can therefore be considered as a dynamic development of architectural direction to meet the challenges of rapid urbanisation and development in the Asian emerging economies. It should become an important milestone in establishing the intellectual status of the province in relation to the dominance of the metropolis.

---

1. David Harvey. 1989. *The Condition of Post Modernity: an enquiry into the origins of cultural change.* Oxford: Blackwell.
2. Rem Koolhaas and Brice Mau. 1995. *S, M, L, XL.* Rotterdam: The Monacelli Press, Inc.

REINVIGORATING TRADITION
EVOKING THE VERNACULAR

REINVENTING TRADITION
THE SEARCH FOR NEW PARADIGMS

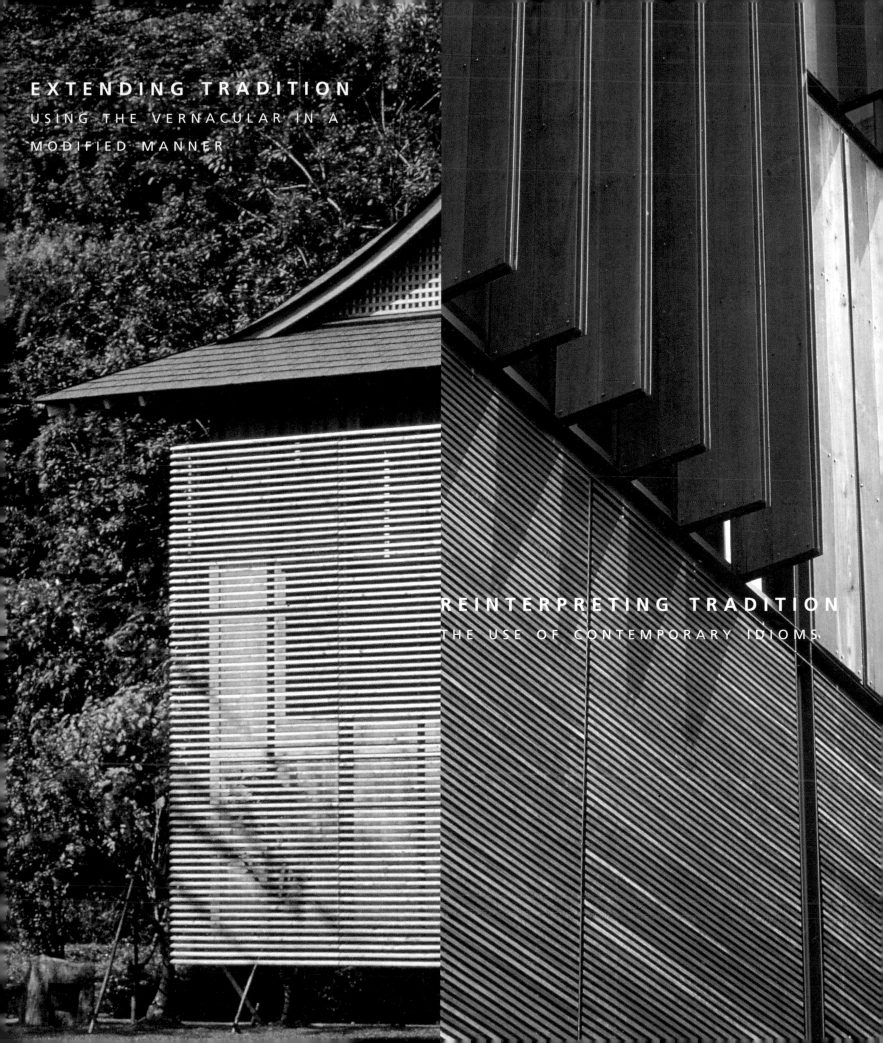

EXTENDING TRADITION
USING THE VERNACULAR IN A
MODIFIED MANNER

REINTERPRETING TRADITION
THE USE OF CONTEMPORARY IDIOMS

CHAPTER 4

REINVIGORATING TRADITION

EVOKING THE VERNACULAR

Currently, buildings around the world are rarely created by craftsmen. Traditional forms no longer represent how buildings are now being constructed. In traditional architecture, the logic of construction was visually apparent to everyone – the architecture directly represented the materials used and the method of construction employed. It simultaneously incorporated technical and significative norms. However, these "transparent" technologies are gradually being displaced by the evolution of material science. Quality is not judged by the skill of fabrication, but more by the skill of installation. Workmanship is valued above craftsmanship. Figuration in architecture hence becomes less to do with a response to materials and more to do with the associative attributes of particular shapes and forms.

In Southeast Asian societies, architects caught in the throes of rapid transformation are learning how to cope with the modernisation and homogenisation that modern building techniques appear to produce. Issues of self, regional and national identities, as well as cultural continuity and the so-called dichotomy between modernity and tradition are well debated. The issue of symbolic meanings in contemporary architecture raises further questions, and remains critical in understanding how an architecture that aspires to evoke traditions in various manifestations operates in these societies.

Modern mass tourism has important social consequences for nearly all societies. It is based on two contradictory phenomena: on the one hand, a global homogenisation of the culture of the tourists, and on the other, the preservation of local ethnic groups and attractions for tourist consumption.

To attract the ever-increasing number of tourists, entrepreneurs and tour operators often use traditions and heritage, both authentic and manufactured, for mass consumption. Holiday resorts are building types that are precisely tailored to fulfil this need. Being intrinsically contrived, many of them are now, paradoxically, being marketed for their architectural merits, which are hailed for their "authenticity". For example, the principals of Wimberly Allison Tong & Goo, an architectural firm that specialises in resort design, claim that "WAT & G

went on to create hundreds of successful projects over the next five decades, all the while heeding the principle of cultural authenticity."[1]

David Harvey has criticised the emergence of the "simulacrum" in Post-Modern culture as being: *"a state of such near perfect replication that the difference between the original and the copy becomes almost impossible to spot ... With modern building materials it is possible to replicate ancient buildings with such exactitude that authenticity or origins can be put into doubt."*[2]

The currently popular

art of appropriation is explored by Thomas Lawson in his article "Nostalgia as Resistance in Modern Dreams". He writes that: *"No matter where we look, it is becoming increasingly difficult to recognise an original from a copy, or from a copy of a copy. Mimicry has replaced innovation as a creative value. We recycle everything."* [3]

This search for instantaneous impact also gives rise to a perceived loss of depth. Jameson describes contemporary cultural production's fixation with appearances as "contrived depthlessness". History and cultural forms are commercialised. Hewison claims that *"Post-Modernism and the heritage industry are linked ... Both conspire to create a shallow screen that intervenes between our present lives, our history. We have no understanding of history in depth, but instead are offered a contemporary creation, more costume drama and re-enactment than critical discourse."* [4] Through the media, architectural styles from the past are viewed as an archive to be raided in order to achieve historical legitimacy.

The effects of tourism have been ubiquitous. As we move into a new epoch of global culture, tourist amenities, in particular, have developed in response to these new influences. In many parts of the Third World the "international standard" hotel, whether privately owned, or owned by the state but run by an international hotel chain, is one of the most conspicuous symbols of modernity. Such buildings continue to propagate the isolationist tendency of tourist architecture. Besides affecting the definitions of "tradition" and "modern", they are also involved in redefining "authenticity" within the culture involved.

Studies have suggested that tourism drastically transforms the very places that tourists go to see. This has led to a "romanticising" of areas in the life of the host culture, particularly in terms of the local customs, rituals, festivals and the arts. Such perceived commodification allegedly changes the meaning of cultural products as well as of human relations.

However, there is relatively little literature available on the significance and impact of tourist architecture. In the *Report from the Master Jury of the Aga Khan Awards 1986*, the Award Jury *"considered that the provision of tourist amenities did have important educational, culture-bridging and economic benefits. The design of buildings for tourism was felt to involve quite different criteria from those involved in assessing any other architectures."* [5]

In many parts of Asia, exquisite works that tangibly draw their contents from traditional sources are proliferating. These works, because of their exquisite craftsmanship and understated proffering of luxury, are further challenging the debate of cultural authenticity. Although based on a traditionalist approach, they are not tacky versions of skin-deep treatments of indigenous archetypes. They are distinguished from the arbitrary kitsch agglomeration of vernacular details. Rather, what they display is a genuine reinvigoration of traditional craft wisdom.

This admiration for the vernacular has resulted in the perpetuation of an architectural language that assumes the status of authenticity through ensuring a perceived historical continuity. In the words of Karsten Harries, *"... buildings that deserve to be called works of architecture ... do indeed represent ... other buildings that tradition has endowed with a special aura, perhaps because they are associated with a more original and presumably more genuine dwelling. Representing such buildings, works of architecture at the same time represent themselves, drawing from the aura of the represented buildings a special significance for themselves."* [6]

1. Wimberly Allison Tong & Goo. 1995. *The Hospitality And Leisure Architecture of Wimberly Allison Tong & Goo*, Rockport Publishers, Inc., p. 6.
2. David Harvey. 1992. *The Condition of Postmodernism. An Inquiry into the Origins of Social Change.* Cambridge, Mass. and Oxford: Blackwell, p. 289.
3. Thomas Lawson. 1988. "Nostalgia as Resistance" in *Modern Dreams — The Rise and Fall and Rise of Pop.* Cambridge, Mass: The MIT Press, p. 163.
4. R. Hewison. 1987. *The Heritage Industry,* London: Methuen London, p. 135.
5. Ismail Serageldin. 1989. "The Aga Khan Award for Architecture" in *Space For Freedom: The Search For Architectural Excellence in Muslim Societies,* London: Butterworth Architecture, p.72.
6. Karsten Harries. 1988. "Representation and Re-Presentation in Architecture", *VIA*, No. 9, The Graduate School of Fine Arts, University of Pennsylvania, p. 18.

NOVOTEL BENOA

BALI, INDONESIA. 1996

BUNNAG ARCHITECTS, THAILAND

The hotel is composed with a delightful series of carefully orchestrated spaces linked by steps and level changes.

In this age of unconstrained mobility, globally the most rapidly developing tourism region is East Asia and the Pacific area, whose rapid economic development has stimulated an unprecedented scale of travel. Especially in Bali, resorts are still being built at a furious pace.

Ever since the island's arguably most imitated resort – the Amandari – hit the resort scene in Southeast Asia, many new 6-star resorts have been designed with the same astutely crafted material richness that is both refined and elegant, sometimes almost to the point of being minimalist. Many new players who have recently jumped onto the boutique resort bandwagon are continuing to build resorts that are a further affirmation of the established pattern. Even in the lower-star categories of hotels, a perceivably similar style is emerging.

Architects of such works are producing an architectural ensemble that is environmentally tuned as well as possessing a sensual refinement and a sure sense of place. These well crafted resorts are generally delightful syntheses of simple materiality and space.

The Novotel Benoa is an interesting addition to the lower-star category of resort architecture because, although it shares many of the concepts and ideas found

The reception lobby is a simple, spacious area animated by precisely detailed timber screens.

in the already well-accepted pattern, it differs, at the same time, in the manner in which its architectural proportion and vocabulary are explored. Designed by Thai architect Mathar Lek Bunnag, the hotel is a multi-faceted, enticing project that defies easy categorisation. Turning against the established precept of "less-is-more", it expresses itself intensely in a highly effusive and celebratory manner.

Located on the fringes of Nusa Dua, beside the Tanjung Benoa Beach, the Novotel offers a Balinese-village atmosphere by using the traditional thatched roof. Individual guest rooms in standard blocks are compact, but well designed. These 180 rooms are spread over small but lushly landscaped gardens. There are also 12 beach cabanas, each with its own private garden as well as the ubiquitous open-air bath tub, now a feature of almost every Balinese resort.

The resort is divided into two portions by the approach road, so that the accommodation is built on two parcels of land. A simple porte cochere leads to the reception lobby, which is spacious but detailed with simple features. Architecturally, the details are Balinese in both inspiration and execution. They exploit an already well-

established vocabulary of forms. Similarly, a veneration of wood is maintained. The roof truss displays the tectonic intricacy found in traditional Balinese structures, with wooden columns resting on tapered concrete bases. Huge but finely laced lattice screens add a sense of enclosure to this open structure, which is connected to the restaurant block behind by open sided linkways.

A touch of whimsy pervades the entire composition. Swerving from the reticence and austerity of many recently completed hotels, the Novotel veers ostensibly towards providing an architectural backdrop that is designed to be fun, witty and relaxed. Bunnag's deft assembly of materials – timber in particular – gives this seemingly insouciant creation a light and uplifting touch,

The careful placement of sculpted objects throughout the grounds enhance the effect of the lush vegetation.

Preceding pages: An open-air amphitheatre, surrounded by the restaurant and other semi-covered public spaces, is the focal point of the composition.

further accentuated by the landscape details which are even more stage-set like in their use of whimsical elements.

The varied and manifold delights of the gardens and the three swimming pools – designed by Bill Bensley of Bensley Design Group – are a pleasure to experience. Tropical vegetation is celebrated throughout the grounds in a manner that can perhaps be best described as one of "unbridled enthusiasm". This lush tropical environment is full of little surprises and idiosyncratic touches. The careful placement of sculptural artefacts – such as enlarged pineapple motifs and female figurines in various poses – enhance the overall effect. At every turn, these unexpected objects in the nooks and crannies of the grounds and poolside surprise and amuse. They blend with the architecture as a coherent statement.

In the final analysis, the Novotel, in reinvigorating tradition, veers perilously close to a theme-park setting. However, the architectural control is undeniable, and the scheme has been thought through in all aspects. Proportion and details are handled in a truly tectonic sense, as opposed to the "architecture" of paper-thin embellishments and fake materials. Without doubt this project sets a new precedent, and certainly generates debates on issues related to the reinvigoration of tradition and its place in the discourse of architecture.

Left: Timber columns rest on tapered concrete bases. Finely detailed timber screens create a
sense of enclosure while maintaining visual links with other areas of the hotel.
Below: The reception lobby. The proportions of architectural elements are handled in a refined
and elegant manner.

Site plan of the entire complex.

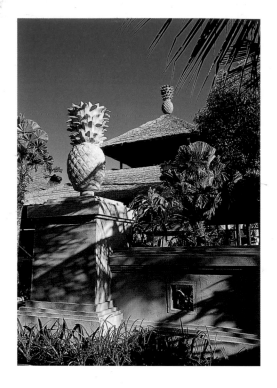

Right: A lap pool is enclosed by a multi-faceted stone wall and delightful water features.

Above: Artefacts and scuptured objects add a touch of whimsy to the landscaped gardens.
Below: The amphitheatre is defined by a series of different floor finishes, level changes and torch pedestals.

TEAHOUSE

SHANGHAI, CHINA. LATE 70'S

FENG JIZHONG, CHINA

Above: A study model of the Teahouse
Top Right: Set amidst a tranquil garden, the
Teahouse blends into the surroundings.

The Square Pagoda Garden lies about 30 km southwest of Shanghai and to the east of Songjiang County. Designed in the late '70s by Feng Jizhong, it is an interesting garden that integrates classical Chinese precedents and modern influences. The end result is a distinctive garden with its own verve which also evokes a strong vernacular flavour of the region south of the Yangtze River.

The original site was barren except for the presence of a ruined pagoda built in the early North Song Dynasty (960-1279 AD), a ruined screen wall built in the Ming Dynasty (1368-1647 AD) and a stone bridge built in the Yuan Dynasty (1206-1368 AD). Feng decided to integrate these artifacts into the design of the garden. Conceptually, the *parti* was to mix the old and new in a juxtaposition that would enhance each other.

Two classical buildings from the old districts of Shanghai were moved into the garden, and a few new structures were also designed to form key pieces of the overall composition. These include two gateways, a restaurant, a teahouse, several pavilions and rambling covered path-ways. Traditional elements of classical Chinese garden design – such as spacious squares, meadows, boulevards and bridges – were integrated into the Square Pagoda Gar-

The organic form of the roof is the most evocative part of the design.

den. At the same time, the Square Pagoda Garden was also conceived as an open-air museum. The new additions, although inspired by traditional forms, were designed to evoke contemporary influences. "The Helouxian Teahouse" is of special significance. Here, the technique of bamboo and timber construction is a primary determinant of form. Situated at the southeast corner of the Garden, the Teahouse is a simple bamboo structure supporting a huge thatched roof.

Hailed by many critics for its ingenious integration of traditional form with a modern conception of space, the Teahouse is ostensibly influenced by the architectural styles of the vernacular houses of Songjiang County. Traditional houses in the region have distinctive roofs which slope in four directions with ridges shaped like the curve of an ox's horn, and these qualities are evident in the Teahouse.

Similarly, the ground beneath the roof is designed in three overlapping levels paved with large square bricks. A series of curved walls serve to enclose both the internal spaces as well as the external courtyards. The conception of these walls is distinctly modern; they integrate the interior with the exterior in a seamless manner.

The interior has a truly appealing verve which is the result of Feng's ability to exploit the immediacy of bamboo. While the dexterous spatial moves are finely judged, the attention the architect lavishes on details and joints compels greater admiration. Bamboo columns, supported by steel bowls, are painted white while the knobs of the bamboo rods that cross one another have a coat of black paint.

There is a wonderful ambience of reflective repose, making the place an ideal environment suited for contemplation, just like it is in a traditional teahouse. Together with all the other architectural pieces in the composition, the Square Pagoda Garden is a modern Chinese garden that is deeply rooted to its past.

Close-up view of the roof structure

NATIONAL CRAFTS MUSEUM

DELHI, INDIA. 1975–90

CHARLES CORREA, INDIA

Indian architect Charles Correa occupies a special niche among the small group of distinguished Asian architects who have achieved international acclaim. For his enlightened contribution to architecture, Correa has received many awards, including the 1987 Gold Medal of the Indian Institute of Architects and the 1990 Gold Medal of the International Union of Architects. Correa's achievements received further recognition in 1994 with the award of the prestigious Praemium Imperiale.

Correa has developed a truly unique architectural style that is distinguished by two traits: it shows great reverence and respect for tradition as well as climate. His works can also be seen as an integration of outdoor and indoor spaces, and in particular, "open-to-sky" spaces, an example of which are his courtyards. These are Correa's favourite elements because he firmly believes that they satisfy some kind of primordial instinct in man.

"In a poor country like India", Correa once wrote, "we simply cannot afford to squander the kind of resources required to air-condition a glass tower under the tropical sun. And that, of course, is an advantage, for it means that the building itself must, through its very form, create the 'controls' the user needs."

The rich crafts of India are arranged in a series of beautiful courtyards linked by a central "open-to-sky" pathway.

Right: Art and architecture blend seamlessly in this integrated complex.

Below: The "ritualistic pathway" concept was used in the Museum's layout.

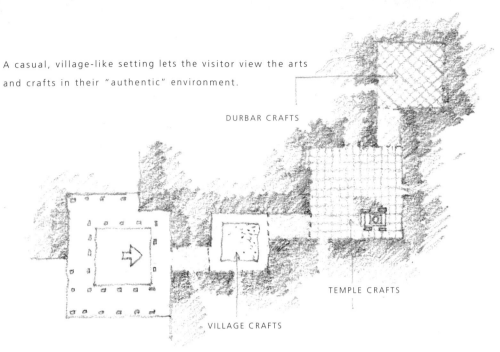

DURBAR CRAFTS

TEMPLE CRAFTS

VILLAGE CRAFTS

In Correa's book *The Ritualistic Pathway: 5 Projects – A Portfolio of Architecture*, the title itself comes from a pervasive theme found in his strongly conceptual works. Inspired by the monumental temples of India, which are experienced as a movement through the sacred open-to-sky spaces lying between them, Correa sees this movement as an important ritualistic pathway, a *pradakshina* – "a movement through the sacred open-to-sky spaces ... towards a sacred centre." The various architectural manifestations of this pathway are found in all his projects.

The National Crafts Museum in New Delhi manifests the idea of using climate as a generator of form as well as the *parti* of the ritualistic pathway. India's rich crafts are arranged in a series of beautiful courtyards linked by a central open-to-sky pathway – Correa's metaphor for the Indian street – the way they have been laid out all through the ages: in a village-like environment. The casual setting allows the visitor to meander through the complex , while enjoying *enfilade* views across the series of spaces. The exhibits get larger towards the end of the sequence and the route terminates on a roof garden which forms an amphitheatre for folk dances while also serving as an open-air display area for large handicrafts.

The museum's core collection of over 25, 000 items of folk and tribal art, crafts and textiles also serves as an important archive and reference collection for traditional craftsmen. Honed carefully for its users needs, the building has been continually upgraded and, as the Director, Dr Jyotindra Jain, says, is "a flexible building ... as an Indian village street would be flexible..."

While deeply conscious of history, Correa nonetheless views mere imitation of the past not as a solution, but as only a pastiche. To him, this is a process of superficial "Transfer", where imagery from other sources are transferred "without any care whatsoever for the profound mythic values from which [they] sprang." His abiding insistence that good architecture should seek transformation, where the issues and principles of ancient iconography are understood and then reinterpreted to suit contemporary needs, is admired by many.

In the Museum, Correa has tangibly drawn from the vernacular and other traditional sources. At the same time, he has fused new ideas and Modernist idioms – such as the use of an orthogonal grid in ordering the spaces – and in the process, transformed them into a building that vigorously resonates with the past.

Fragments of actual buildings form part of the exhibits.

HOUSE AT SWISS CLUB ROAD

SINGAPORE. 1997

ERNESTO BEDMAR, SINGAPORE

Set in an exclusive landscape of palatial private residences, this detached house exhibits a marked tectonic sensibility. Designed by Singapore-based Argentinean architect Ernesto Bedmar of Bedmar & Shi Designs, this project is a superb demonstration of the practice's propensity for seeking strong spatial solutions. At the same time, it extends the repertoire of forms associated with Bedmar & Shi's impressive oeuvre.

Highly animated by an interplay of solidity and transparency, colour and light, this house is the product of deft hands and sure eyes. Horizontal movement through the house is an important design consideration. The entrance is screened by an imposing wall whose starkness and sheer height appear, at first sight, disconcerting. There are obvious traces of Latin American architecture here.

On "piercing" this screen, however, the visitor is taken into a totally different experience. The entrance hallway is designed on a strong visual axis that links the house from the front to the rear. Space folds and enfolds as one moves through the house, revealing views and extending perceptions.

Designing with an organisational simplicity in mind, the architect breaks down the artificial separation of inside from outside, thus creating one of the more highly successful features of the house. The basic blocks of accommodation are clustered around a swimming pool and lushly landscaped courtyards. The use of water adds to the resort-like ambiance, while the careful siting of the blocks make the house as well as the site appear much larger than they actually are.

Having meticulously resolved the pragmatic concerns,
Bedmar's inclination for the expressive honesty of natural materials is also evident. The honed simplicity of
details and the understanding of materiality result in a
tactile architecture that thrills the senses and allows for
a full scale of experiences. Careful detailing and the clean,
controlled execution of luxurious finishes ensure a thoroughly pleasant interior layout. However, different parts
of the house present different characteristics. For example, the use of salvaged columns from other countries in
the region, as well as the adaptation of colonial-style
columns add an eclectic touch to the house.

Bedmar's luxurious houses chart an architectural territory
which reflects preoccupations with re-definitions of the
vernacular forms of the region, as well as the romance
of tropical living. His work rejects the idea that the
vernacular is pure, scenographic, picturesque and hence
stagnant. Instead, he draws on the notion of improvisa-
tion and hence refined development.

Critics have pointed out that Bedmar's works have
not deviated much from an appropriated, and still
visibly Balinese idiom. But this project must be seen as
part of an evolving, rather than an evolved oeuvre. The

Ornamental columns are part of the architectural vocabulary.

innovative use of traditional materials has certainly been taken much further. The idea of a heavy base and a light top – capped by a "floating" roof with deep over-hangs – is also executed in an interesting and delightful manner. At the same time, this is a lucid work, one where the experiential aspects are of greater significance than its imagery of the romantic ideal.

Permeated with light, the entire house reverberates with a certain luminosity and brightness. It is an eloquent reminder of the attractiveness of light in architecture. Nevertheless, its most outstanding quality is perhaps the way spaces flow from the indoors to the outdoors, while blending intangible qualities of the tropics into a delightful mix.

Openings laid out in an axial manner accentuate the depth of view.

Intimate courtyards provide an atmosphere conducive to repose and contemplation.

CHAPTER 5

REINVENTING TRADITION

THE SEARCH FOR NEW PARADIGMS

"To rob a people of its tradition is to rob it of inborn strength and identity. To rob a people of opportunity to grow through invention or through acquisition of values from other races is to rob it of its future."

– Frederick Douglas and Rene d' Harnoncourt

The Report of the Master Jury for the Aga Khan Awards argues that *"in traditional societies, age-old architectural forms have reached such a state of high sophistication that even as they may slowly degenerate they remain more expressive and sympathetic to the aspirations of the people than all but the most perceptive of contemporary designs. Particularly in the hands of local craftsmen, the expressions of these surviving traditions sometimes have a vigour and conviction which truly celebrate devotion, contemplation or commemoration."* [1]

Many scholars have rejected the definition of tradition as a set of fixed attributes. It is a series of layers transformed over time. Hobsbawn used the term "invented tradition" to include both traditions that are actually invented, con-structed and formally instituted and those that emerge in a less easily defined manner within a short time frame.[2] He defines the term as *"taken to mean a set of practices, normally governed by overtly or tacitly accepted rules and of a ritual or symbolic nature, which seek to inculcate certain values and norms of behaviour by repetition, which automatically implies continuity with the past. In fact, where possible, they normally attempt to establish continuity with a suitable historic past."* [3]

Within the vast variety of multi-faceted traditions are the repositories of history and the intricate fabric of myths and symbols which can be tapped creatively. Many practitioners have advocated an approach based on using elements of the past and combining them in new ways. The Egyptian

architect Hassan Fathy, for example, introduced new elements and borrowed proportions from elsewhere in his New Gourna Village. His attempt to create a new community was a failure, because it had no economic base. His concern was primarily with the creation of a form based on an invented tradition. Vaults and domes were borrowed and combined with mud structures that Fathy assumed might have been used by the indigenous traditions.

Although the New Gourna Village failed to become a feasible village community, Fathy's work has, nonetheless, forced the architectural community to confront the issue of how to represent the identity of a people in its architecture. His work has also had a filtering-down effect, generating a trend towards building such forms. However, by the very fact of having acquired a popular appeal, the critical question now is whether such an invented tradition can be considered a legitimate expression of "Egyptian" identity.

In Asia, the resort industry has once again spawned a number of exciting progenies in this category. Elements of the past have been combined with those from other traditional source outside its cultural context. Although the very idea might seem to be an abomination, in the hands of a skilled designer the results bring a new vigour of their own, and introduce more variables into the equation, despite the debatable issue of validity.

It must be remembered, however, that throughout history there have been discontinuities in architectural traditions. Architectural forms are not immutable. They have never remained stagnant as a "pure" culture. There have always been hybrids of indigenous and imported types. These linked series of precedents are part of the creative process of cross-fertilisation. They have been diffused, hybridised, and in the process, synergised. Each in turn has become a potential model for generating even more transformations. However, in traditional societies cultural processes and external forces took a long time to reach states which could be considered "established". Once established, though, these paradigms were sustained for similarly long periods of time.

In Asia, European colonialism in the 19th Century resulted in new paradigm shifts that were imposed, almost literally, overnight. An unequal socio-economic and cultural exchange resulted in the emergence of "re-invented" traditions. In the process of stripping away local cultural identities, certain types of hybrid architecture and urban forms emerged, and eventually gained acceptance. The colonial bungalows of Malaysia and Singapore, for instance, are good examples of the colonists' architectural imports drawing lessons from the traditional Malay house. Alien imports of new building types were also adapted to local contexts. The term "invention of tradition" is derived from Eric Hobsbawn and Terence Ranger, who edited a book which argues that a colonial power had to invent "tradition" in order to create a sense of historical legitimacy.

Raymond Williams points out that what may pass off as "cultural traditions" or "the significant past" are actually *selective* traditions:

"From a whole possible area of past and present, certain meanings and practices are chosen for emphasis, certain other meanings and practices are neglected and excluded. ... Some of these meanings and practices are

reinterpreted, diluted, or put into forms which support or at least do not contradict other elements within the effective dominant culture." [4]

Hence, traditions are always contested, transformed, resisted and invented.

Today hybridisation is seen as an important constituent of the sense of cultural identity and architectural tradition. The latter is now accepted as an ongoing process that is fluid – one that changes over the course of time – and inevitably dictated by circumstances of place and programme. The question is – what impact will the compression of time and space by communication technology have on issues concerning the representation and evocation of tradition within architectural forms?

1. Ismail Serageldin. 1989. "The Aga Khan Award for Architecture" in *Space For Freedom : The Search For Architectural Excellence in Muslim Societies,* London: Butterworth Architecture, p.71.
2. Eric Hobsbawm. 1983. "Introduction: Inventing Traditions" in *The Invention of Tradition,* ed. Eric Hobsbawm and Terence Ranger, Cambridge: Cambridge University Press, p.1.
3. Ibid.
4. Raymond Williams. 1980. *Problems in materialism and culture,* London: New Left Books, p. 39.

KANDAWGYI PALACE HOTEL

YANGON, MYANMAR. 1996

BUNNAG ARCHITECTS, THAILAND

The potential for the development of tourism in Southeast Asia is immense, but the unabated wave of hotel construction in the region has continued to produce many buildings that are drearily homogenous. One of the most conspicuous symbols of modernity in many parts of the region is the "international standard" hotel. This is especially so in the rapidly developing countries of Indochina.

Myanmar, in particular, is experiencing a phenomenal growth in its tourist trade. Being the largest country in mainland Southeast Asia, and also being blessed with a large diversity of natural scenery as well as superb architecture, the country is currently witnessing the construction of many tourism projects. However, many of them are designed in the same Neo-Classical kitsch that has become a blight to all Asian cities. Ill-proportioned and adorned with ridiculous and irrelevant ornamentation, these buildings have an inevitable tendency to homogeneity behind their dressed-up facades. Soaked in nostalgia and often couched in the plaintive term of "tradition", many offer a superficial reassurance of being well-crafted buildings. However, although they suggest a thoroughly absorbing sensual physicality, there is little creative reinterpretation of regional history.

56 | 57

Aerial view of the hotel complex and its adjoining private villas.

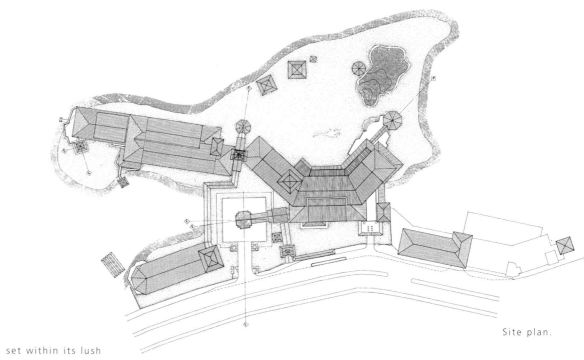

Site plan.

Viewed from across the lake, the hotel, set within its lush green surroundings, presents an imposing facade.

View of the porte cochere from the reception lobby.

This is perhaps best summed up by David Klob, who argues that *"traditional vocabularies might be used and metaphorically changed in ways that affirm a solidarity that is not that of shared immediate belief, a solidarity that remains comfortable with future reinterpretation. There is room for buildings that are neither naive celebrations nor elitist games."*

One of the rare few that demonstrates an attempt at a creative reinterpretation of the country's rich architectural heritage is the Kandawgyi Palace Hotel in the capital city of Yangon. Designed by Thai architect Lek Bunnag, the exactingly executed hotel offers a sensual physicality that is thoroughly absorbing.

Bunnag himself is acutely sensitive to the cultural complexities of Southeast Asia. His Harvard graduate thesis, "Conservation of Meaning", which received a distinction from the university, reflects his long standing interest in architectural projects that embody cultural heritage. Together with landscape architect Bill Bensley, Bunnag has collaborated on many resorts in Southeast Asia. These include the Pangkor Laut resort in Malaysia and the Novotel Benoa in Bali.

The client, Bijoux Holdings, requested a 5-storey tall building, and the architectural resolution aims at visually balancing a strong horizontal expression with elegant, multi-tiered roofs. As the design is based on surviving traditional skills, the building invariably needed the involvement of craftsmen from an early stage. The result is a well-crafted resort that, despite its 200-room size, is a tribute to fine artisanry.

Viewed from the opposite shore of a serene lake, the building provides an interesting silhouette. Though imposing, the Kandawgyi Palace Hotel sits very well on its site. The rhythm of the multi-tiered roofs offsets the rigidity of the guest room elevation. In addition, the use of timber shingles for the roof provides a sense of rusticity and serenity to the overall massing.

The entire entrance porch is built in golden teak, using traditional Burmese wood construction methods. Its high-volume space immediately sets a tone of controlled grandeur. Closely placed columns in the reception lobby accentuate the sense of vertiginous space. At the same time, it is tangibly evident that the architectural vocabulary of Myanmar has been intensively explored in a thoroughly celebratory manner. Forms are drawn from the traditional architecture of Indochina

Right: The eclecticism and studied complexity of the architecture – rare in the region's prevailing resort architectural style – is carried off with panache.

and juxtaposed, composed and reinterpreted in a highly refreshing manner. Scale is handled in a sensitive way, such that the building retains an intimate feel.

Impeccable craftsmanship, apparent throughout the development, is a constant pleasure to look at. Ornate eave carvings, richly patterned gable screens and other decorative motifs are hand-crafted by local artisans and integrated into the design. The ancient Burmese plaster-painted flower wall element, for example, is used to envelop the entrance car porch. Its sheer whiteness sets up an interesting juxtaposition with the darkly-stained timber structures.

By setting the building back from the main road, Bunnag has also allowed the hotel to achieve a greater sense of presence. Existing mature trees have been preserved, hence blending the hotel into its site. The result is a handsomely detailed resort where site, form and materials have been integrated into an indissoluble whole.

It cannot be denied, however, that the eclecticism and studied complexity of the design are likely to be the source of issues of contention among critics and architects who may question the bricolaged aesthetic of the project. Again, however, in our opinion this project's

tectonic rigour is undeniable. The building's innate vigour is obvious. In the final analysis, this deftly articulated building has been achieved with a panache unique to the resort industry of the region. The Kandawgi Palace Hotel, in making an enlivening contribution to the resort scene, also succinctly raises several pertinent issues related to notions of quotation and invention.

Faced with an increasingly sophisticated clientele, hotel developers, forced to look beyond the mere provision of room and recreation, are beginning to realise that architecture can make that big difference. As architect Christopher Alexander once noted, "There is no perfect static language, which once defined, will stay defined forever. No language is ever finished." The architecture of Kandawgyi Palace Hotel, through its earnest attempt, certainly points towards a possible direction.

Rich tones of natural timber are highlighted by the shifting play of light.

MIYAGI SANT JUAN BAUTISTA MUSEUM

MIYAGI, JAPAN. 1993

KAZUHIRO ISHII, JAPAN

Traditional timber elements and steel-and-glass structures are intriguingly juxtaposed.

Designed by Kazuhiro Ishii, the Miyagi Sant Juan Bautista Museum houses the artifacts and all other forms of documentation of the 17th Century ship called the *Miyagi Sant Juan Bautista* which transported Japan's first ever delegation to Europe.

The 180-member group of the Keichou Delegation, headed by Tsunenaga Hasekura, was despatched to Europe by Masamune Date, and the ship, a huge wooden structure specially designed for this journey, set sail from Tsukinoura in the Ojika Peninsula in 1631.

In 1993, a little over 360 years after her maiden voyage to Europe, the 55-metre long and 50-meter high ship was rebuilt. The Miyagi Sant Juan Bautista Museum was designed specifically to showcase the ship, which is its central focus. Conceptually, the building was meant to take a secondary role to the surrounding landscape of undulating hills and the nearby sea.

Existing contours provided the initial design inspiration. The exhibition hall and the entrance hall were designed as subterranean structures, with the roof of the exhibition hall forming a green plaza on the ground level, providing unobstructed view of the ship, the sea and the verdant hillsides. Like the sinuous simplicity

Top Right: The position of the building, its relationship to the ship and the sea, have been carefully studied.
Below: The sinuous curves of the building are contextual responses to the hill contours.

Above: Simple geometrical patterns are created by the timber roof elements.
Right: Timber roof details provide an intricate layering of internal spaces.

of the external form, the internal planning and circulation are simple and logical. A large staircase rising from the green plaza links it to the entrance lobby, which is fully glazed. The *Sant Juan Bautista* is hence visible from all the important spaces.

A conscious articulation of parts results in a tectonically expressive structure imbued with the architect's characteristic aplomb and confidence. The gently curved plan of the exhibition hall is tucked into the geographical features of the undulating hills. The exhibition dock, with its views directed towards the sea, is built against a series of retaining walls. A 2-metre-wide glass edge along the roof ensures that the top of the ship's mast is visible from all vantage points.

Permeated by light and scenes of nature, this sensuously sculptured structure is an eloquent reminder of the delight of transparency in architecture. It engages on a highly visceral level. The delicately robust architectural language is shrewdly developed by exploiting the constructional logic of timber and steel-and-glass detailing. The structure, floor, interior walls and ceiling are all built of wood, echoing the early boat-building traditions associated with the ship. Drawing from both traditional Japanese boat-building and timber construction techniques, Ishii has superbly demonstrated a crafting and grafting of associated technologies and skills into a coherent whole.

JAWAHAR KALA KENDRA

JAIPUR, INDIA. 1986–92

CHARLES CORREA, INDIA

Respected as a strong proponent of cultural rootedness, Indian architect Charles Correa has always maintained that architecture must address issues beyond the purely empirical and functional, and instead tackle meaning and symbolism in new and profound ways. To him, *"architecture matters as an art because it's the barometer of the health of a society – and a measure of its view of itself."*

In one of his usual epigrammatic statements, Correa argues that *"we must understand our past well enough to value it – and yet also well enough to know why (and how) it must be changed. Architecture is not just a reinforcement of values – social, political, economic. On the contrary, it should open new doors – to new aspirations."*

The Jawahar Kala Kendra is an Arts Centre in Jaipur, dedicated to Pandit Jawaharlal Nehru, India's first Prime Minister. Designed by Charles Correa, the building, inspired by a series of dualities, is created in a style the architect termed "double-coded". The concept is drawn from a metaphorical interpretation of the city of Jaipur, as well as from two key personalities – Maharaja Jai Singh and Nehru.

Jai Singh – the ruler who built Jaipur and the city's renowned Jantar Mantar Astronomical Observatory – was

The building is enclosed behind 8-metre-high walls clad in red sandstone.

There are nine 30-metre- square components,
each defined by high planar walls.

moved by two sets of mythic ideas – that of the Navgraha Mandala (the "mandala of the nine planets" which was believed to be the origin of Jaipur's plan, with one of the planets being shifted to the opposite corner to avoid an existing hill), and the myths of progress and science.

Correa sees Jai Singh's ability to embrace both past and future simultaneously as analogous to Nehru's. Born more than two centuries after Jai Singh, Nehru guided India's independence in its early years with a keen awareness of the need to embrace both tradition and innovation. The Arts Centre was hence conceptualised as a *"contemporary building based on an archaic notion of the Cosmos: the very same Navgraha Mandala, with one of the squares moved aside, so as to provide a point of entry, and to recall the gesture that created the original plan for Jaipur".*

The architecture is derived from a geometric depiction of the cosmic order. It is based on the ancient Vedic understanding of the cosmos in which the 30-metre square mandala of the nine planets is used to define the enclosure of the museum. Each of the nine squares has a great tectonic presence. It is defined by 8-metre high walls, clad in red Agra sandstone and topped by a coping of beige Dholpur stone. The presence of each of the planets

is represented on the walls by its traditional symbol inlaid in white marble.

On a first viewing, the legibility of the planning is less than apparent. However, an understanding of the *parti* will enable the visitor to comprehend the layout immediately. The programmatic functions are allocated and disposed within the squares according to the mythic qualities associated with each of the planets. For instance, the planet Guru, which symbolises Learning, houses the Library. Other spaces include a museum devoted to the textiles, jewellery and other crafts, as well as studios for traditional artisans, a small performing arts centre, and an experimental theatre.

The central square, as specified in the Vedic texts, is a void representing the "Nothing", which can also be interpreted as "Everything". Formal and ritualistic pathways here allow visitors to experience the monumental spaces of the complex.

Correa's buildings, generated from a deep understanding of space, climate and culture, have brought comfort and joy to many people, while his vision of architecture continues to provide a fertile approach for many Asian architects seeking to reintegrate and transform their

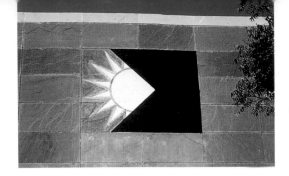

Each of the nine mythic planets is represented by its traditional symbol inlaid in white marble in the red sandstone walls.

respective pasts. Correa firmly believes that *"only a decadent architecture looks obsessively backward. At its most vital, architecture is an agent of change."*

The re-embodiment of ancient iconography in the contemporary context still remains an extremely elusive task for all architects. Correa's works are highly evocative of place. The referential aspects in some of his works are very strong. These exquisitely crafted projects all possess a remarkable combination of the simple and the austere with the complex and the spiritual. A restrained sense of proportion is clearly evident, with the frugal being transformed into something extraordinary and even enigmatic. They all bear witness to a deep conviction in a design ethos that ceaselessly attempts to transform traditions.

Right: A crisp, planar Modernist expression of enclosures is juxtaposed with the strong representation of myths and symbols.

Overleaf: The mural on the wall, painted by traditional Rajasthani artists, is the mythological imagery of Krishna.

Above: The play of light and shadow and the use of an axial layout create an imposing sense of sequential movement.

Right: Interior views and exterior vistas are everywhere framed by rectilinear openings.

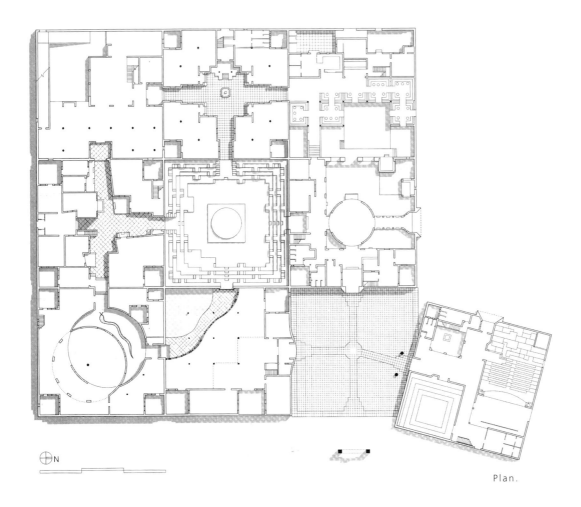

N

Plan.

Reflected images of the complex on glass panel.

BANYAN TREE MALDIVES

VABBINFARU ISLAND, MALDIVES. 1996

ARCHITRAVE DESIGN AND PLANNING, THAILAND

Aerial view of Vabbinfaru Island.

Southeast Asian handicrafts
are used as accent pieces in
the interiors.

The Republic of Maldives has been touted as the world's last remaining island paradise. Its natural attractions of sparkling white beaches and crystal-clear waters, teeming with an abundance of marine life, provide a magnet for tourists.

An archipelago in the Indian Ocean, the Maldives is made up of 26 atolls and some 1,200 gem-like islands, of which only about 200 are inhabited. Under various types of leasehold agreements, more than 70 islands have been set aside exclusively for resort development, thus segregating tourists from the bulk of the indigenous Muslim population.

Each resort is located on a small, uninhabited island – to restrict the perceived negative impact of tourism on the host culture. Apart from the resorts and the capital city of Male, the other islands are out of bounds to tourists.

Set on Vabbinfaru Island, the Banyan Tree Maldives boasts 48 beach front and inland villas. Vabbinfaru, which in Maldivian means "round island circled by a round coral reef", is only 3.5 hectares in size. Accessibility to the island is limited as only small, flat-bottomed barges can navigate the shallow waters. Other constraints

A uniquely designed spiral roof caps each of the 48 villas.

inherent in the project included the unavailability of building materials and skilled workers. These all had to be imported, hence adding to the construction costs. The construction workers came mainly from Indonesia, Singapore, Thailand and India.

Each villa within the Banyan Tree is uniquely designed to reflect the spiral of a seashell. The round shaped building plan and conical thatched roof of the indigenous architecture was adopted as the basis for the villa design. In the Maldives, walls are made from coral, while the thatch is made of *cajan* or coconut leaves. In order to evoke a "sense of traditional Maldivian magic", the architect – Architrave Design and Planning – chose to draw further inspiration from a seashell, specifically the spiral shape of the Chambered Nautilus shell. Every direction of the roof has a different radius, starting from 2.5 metres and gradually increasing to 4.5 metres. This quest for a new and refreshing formal expression is interesting, as it basically reinvents traditions.

The techniques and materials for the roof construction were essentially drawn from Balinese sources. Instead of using *cajan*, Balinese thatch or *alang alang* was used for its neater look as well as its durability. *Alang*

alang is also a very much more flexible material for achieving the conical roof profile. However, the use of the spiral form necessitated a roof construction radically different from traditional Balinese methods. Through a series of trial and error, the use of timber trusses was eradicated and a new structural system devised.

A prefabrication system of construction was used as much as possible. The building components were made in Bali, erected for inspection, and then dismantled again for shipment to the Maldives. This procedure was carried out from the smallest, 25 square-metre building pavilion to the largest 500-plus square-metre pavilion that houses the entertainment centre.

All villas are self-contained, with open terraces and private gardens. They are mainly sited around the edge of the island, for the view. The rooms are not air-conditioned, but the use of adjustable louvres for all openings ensures sufficient cross-ventilation. Huge bathrooms, four-poster beds and recessed sitting areas are typical features of the villas. Further examples of hybridity in the use of objects and materials outside their cultural contexts can be clearly seen in the interior design, in which Asian handicrafts are used as accent pieces.

Above: Huge bathrooms, four-poster beds and recessed sitting areas are provided in every villa.
Right: Though sparse, the interiors of each villa are suitably luxurious.

For instance, the twig laundry basket comes from the Riau Islands south of Singapore, while mango-wood bowls and celadon ceramic vases are sourced from Thailand.

The Front of House is located near the main jetty while the service areas are located in the centre of the island. These larger pavilions, most of which are naturally ventilated, are designed in a polygonal plan. The entertainment centre, with an area of 510 square metres, houses the bar and lounge, a games area, a gallery and a video room. Six steel posts, together with a ring of coconut trunk columns, support its double-tiered roof.

The Banyan Tree is an interesting example of the combination of lessons from different cultures. It has nothing to do with a spurious interpretation of the vernacular. Instead, it reflects an earnest attempt at dealing with the pressures of reinvention, local constraints, as well as the constraints of materials, techniques and economics. The end result combines a coincidence of desire, understanding and method.

CHAPTER 6

EXTENDING TRADITION

USING THE VERNACULAR IN A MODIFIED MANNER

A discernible trend of works which seek out a continuity with local traditions has become apparent in Asia in recent years. These projects either evoke or quote directly from forms and features of past sources. However, in many cases this particularisation of accepted idioms has been internalised. Architects of such works are not overwhelmed by the past. Instead, they are adding to it in an innovative manner, while ostensibly retaining much of the earlier vocabulary.

David Lowenthal argues that *"... there is nothing wrong with such manipulations: difficulties arise only if antiquarian reverence compels us to claim that we are reviving a wholly authentic past, the true version of bygone times that brooks no alternatives. Quite to the con-*

trary, the utility of the past inheres in its many-sidedness, in being all things to all people. It is the flexibility, not the fixity, of the past that makes it so useful in enhancing our sense of ourselves: our interpretations of it alter according to the perspectives and needs of present and future moments." *

Although in most cases attempts at fusing the past with new inventions have resulted in facile eclecticism, nonetheless many interesting works have been built. This approach has been termed either "modern regionalism" or "regionalist modernism" at different times in the recent past. Architects of such works are searching for solutions suited to the complexities of contemporary experience, using available craft technologies.

One prominent exam- ple is Sri Lankan architect Geoffrey Bawa. His works explicitly illustrate the su- perb control he exercises over the use of his coun- try's vernacular structures and its tradition of inher- ited craftsmanship. His be- guiling works of poetry re- sonate within all of us who see them. In a world tee- tering from over-stimula- tion, his exquisite buildings are about modesty, gentle- ness and contemplation. Although a few critics have labelled his architecture as "revivalist", Bawa's corpus of exquisite works is semi- nal for its formal language which seeks inspiration in the traditional building forms and techniques unique to Sri Lanka.

Many architects in Asia have been greatly influenced by Bawa's inimitable works. Many have openly acknowl- edged their debt to him through either their own works or their writings. Shanti Jayawardene, in an essay on Bawa, argues that *"what is critical in his [Bawa's] work is not its indigenous content per se, which in its popular form represents the build- ing mode of the majority. Its significance lies in the act of raising both the formal and the popular indigenous traditions from the degraded status assigned to them in the colonial era, and in the creation from them of a formal architectural language which could once more re- ceive national patronage."*

*David Lowenthal, 1993. "What makes the past matter" in *Companion to Contemporary Architectural Thought*, ed. Ben Farmer and Hentie Louw, London: Routledge, p. 184.

THE ARCHITECT'S HOUSE

COLOMBO, SRI LANKA. 1969

GEOFFREY BAWA, SRI LANKA

Views are carefully framed by openings and lightwells.

Geoffrey Bawa is regarded by many outside the country as the quintessential Sri Lankan architect. His lyrical understanding of space and climate is distilled in the essence of all his works, which are profoundly evocative of tradition.

The large corpus of Bawa's memorable works in Sri Lanka, despite being much imitated, remains enticing and durable through its optimistic reassurance of time-lessness. Though his buildings are all simple and under-stated, they are also enchantingly complex. They have a compelling vitality and regenerative force that are ex-pressed powerfully. The play of space and light demon-strates a rare, sensitive architectural perception. Bawa's projects acquire a patina and a dimension that grow richer with every visit.

One of Bawa's most powerful works is his own resi-dence in Colombo, which is noted for its blend of mo-dern sensibilities and traditional elements, as well as its orchestrated sequence of carefully-composed vistas viewed through courtyards and linkways. The Egyptian architect Hassan Fathy once defined architecture as "the space between the walls and not the walls." To para-phrase the definition, Bawa's architecture is definitely

Every room is directed either towards an intimate landscaped courtyard or a miniature lightwell.

not *about* walls, but about the way light moulds space and reflects *off* walls.

This residence in Bagatelle Road is a lyric statement of light and shadow, where, typical of Bawa, spaces are treated with a poetic intensity. The series of intimate courtyards in the house also illustrate Bawa's conviction that architecture and landscape are an indivisible continuity, even in the context of a dense urban matrix.

Bawa moved into a quarter of the house in 1958. Over the years, four houses were amalgamated into a labyrinth-like complex. Like a mysterious, cryptic maze, the house reveals itself slowly. Views are carefully framed by openings and courtyards, while spaces are richly layered. The interplay of landscape and architecture creates an ambiance of unfolding vistas where framed openings lead the viewer's eye to the most revealing route.

This building's sense of transparency is perhaps best described by Bawa himself: *"For myself a building can only be understood by moving around and through it and by experiencing the modulation and feel of the spaces one moves through – from the outside into verandahs, then rooms, passages, courtyards – the view from these spaces into others, views through to the landscape beyond, and from outside the building, views back through rooms into inner rooms and courts."**

Bawa's house is urban in location, yet rural in spirit. Its richly intimate rooms, with their splendid collection of books, paintings and sculpture, are all directed towards either a delightful courtyard or unbelievably miniature airwells, giving one a sense of engagement with the elements. Bawa's interior architecture is primarily constructed of light itself. Light trickles into rooms seemingly randomly – providing a subtle yet dramatic interplay of light and shade which inspires feelings of great repose.

This residence demonstrates a concern for distilling essentials. It is a virtuoso achievement, succinctly evoking a sense of serenity and security. The allusive voca-bulary of architectural details, manifested through beguiling simplicity, provides indisputable evidence of Bawa's masterly touch.

*Brian Brace Taylor, 1986. *Geoffrey Bawa*. London: Thames and Hudson Ltd. p.18.

Salvaged relics from traditional buildings are
used as parts of the desgn features.

Rooms are richly furnished with exquisite collections of artefacts and art works.

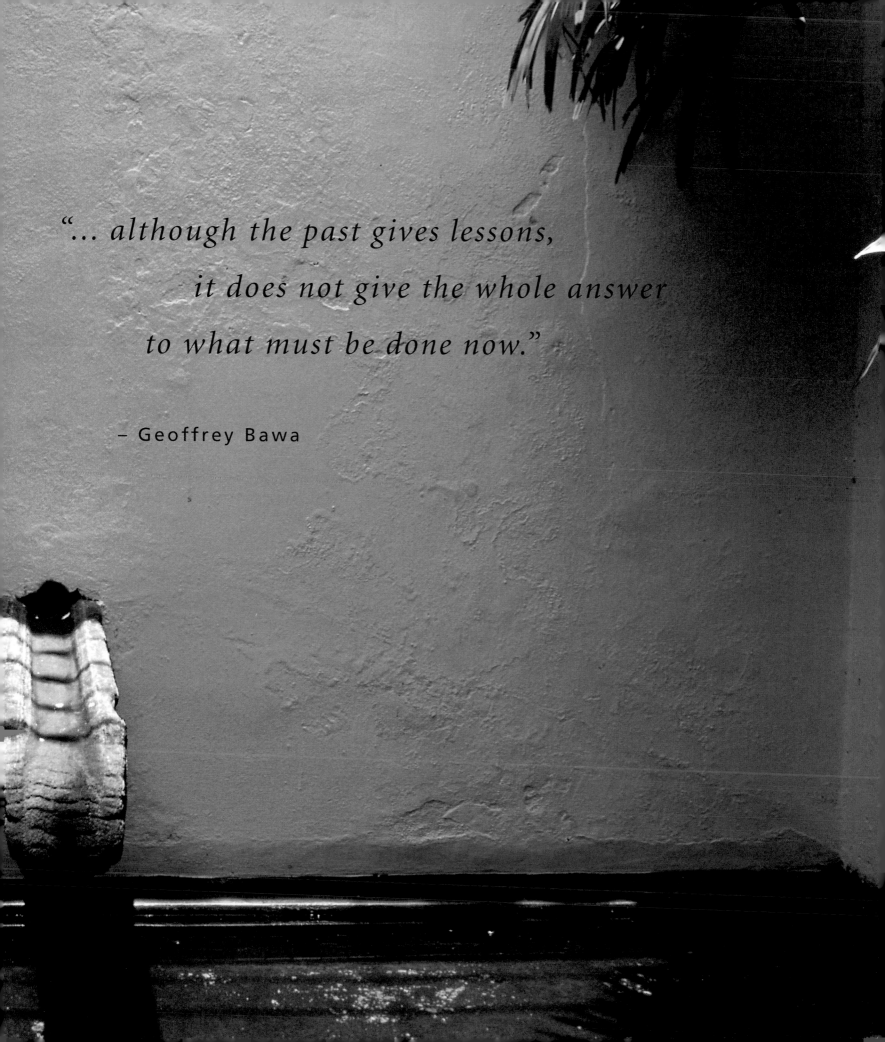

"... although the past gives lessons,
          it does not give the whole answer
      to what must be done now."

– Geoffrey Bawa

Preceding pages: The play of light and shadow imbues the house with a
poetic resonance.
Above: Every object is positioned in an intricate relationship with
architectural elements such as walls and reflecting pools.

The house is a totally introspective labyrinth of interconnected rooms and private courtyards.

INTEGRAL EDUCATION CENTRE

PILIYANDALA, SRI LANKA. 1981

GEOFFREY BAWA, SRI LANKA

The building is carefully inserted into the undulating site in a conscientious effort to exploit the presence of huge trees and wide vistas.

In this enthralling project located on a low hill by the Bolgoda Lake in Piliyandala, Sri Lanka, Geoffery Bawa has skillfully crafted a complex of buildings that gently embrace the undulating landscape. The most outstanding qualities about the building are the way Bawa deals with the dispersion of each individual block on the site, and the manner in which he articulates the series of cascading roofs.

Run by the Catholic Church, the complex was designed as a centre for adult education, for occasional seminars, and also as a holiday retreat. It was financed by Misereor, a West German Roman Catholic aid-giving organisation. The architectural programme includes a multi-purpose hall, accommodation facilities, a library and kitchens.

The site is magnificent. In the hands of Bawa, the building is inevitably a deference to nature. Bawa has respectfully inserted the building into the site to exploit the abundance of trees. When looking at the Education Centre, one has a feeling that the trees are more important than the buildings. Each white-washed block is juxtaposed with the verticality of the slender trees as a picturesque composition.

The proportions of every block are sensitively designed to evoke a sense of rhythm and verticality.

In this building, Bawa deals with the climate through the use of a series of deep overhanging roofs. The construction method is simple, and the preference for elemental architectural expression is evident. Using a system of brick walls and timber-framed roofs, Bawa cleverly exploits the contours of the land to great effect. Roofs cascade across the site in a harmonious manner. The various blocks are carefully proportioned to enhance the effect of the entire complex on the observer.

The Education Centre has an organic and primal quality. An invigorating haven, it is both modest and subtle. Bawa's sureness of touch has created an elegant complex that is imbued with a quiet dignity that, most importantly, is deeply rooted to the culture of Sri Lanka. Amidst the relentless search for novelty and gratuitous imagery so clearly perceivable in contemporary architecture, his buildings restore some semblance of balance. Concerned with adding sensual physicality to life's experience, they form truly sublime settings for the drama of human life.

Bawa once said that "it is impossible to explain architecture in words". That is absolutely true. Architecture must speak for itself, and the architecture of Bawa's buildings certainly speak for themselves – in the most soothing, gentle and eloquent voice possible.

Each block is set within a landscape of towering trees.

Above: A series of stepped walkways connect the various blocks.

Right: Bawa's inventive use of terraced roof forms cascading across the site is probably the project's most potent statement.

Above: Interior view of a classroom.
Right: Viewed from one of the many interconnecting walkways, the complex's integration with the green landscape is a hallmark of the scheme.

BEIJING JU'ER HUTONG

BEIJING, CHINA. 1987 – (ONGOING)

WU LIANGYONG, CHINA

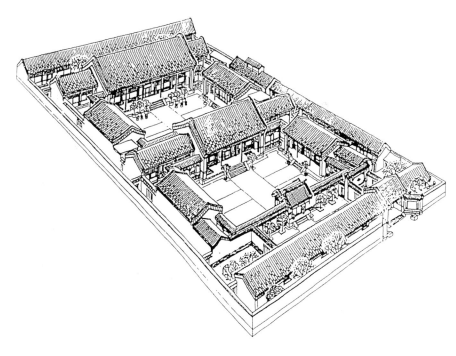

The Ju'er Hutong Courtyard Housing Project in Beijing is an important attempt at transforming the vernacular into a form that is applicable to contemporary needs. Led by the Beijing Municipal Government and Beijing East City District Government, Wu Liangyong was the chief architect for the project.

"Hutong" denotes a traditional urban neighbourhood, and Ju'er Hutong is a typical inner city neighbourhood in Beijing's Eastern City District. The objective of this neighbourhood rehabilitation project was to find new ways to upgrade the physical environment as well as to integrate the necessities of modern living for cultural continuity within the historic city. The old city of Beijing is the finest example of classic Chinese city planning and design, but rapid urbanisation has seriously threatened the existing city environment.

The project, which began in 1987, is an ongoing one which has successfully improved living conditions, but most importantly, it stimulates inspiration for new design patterns for Old City conservation. In the Old City area, the traditional brick-and-timber courtyard houses are increasingly dilapidated, and living conditions inevitably deteriorated after the 1976 Tangshan earthquake.

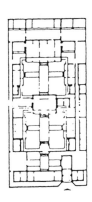

Axonometric view and floor plan of a typical courtyard dwelling.

96 | 97

Above: Traditional motifs are used in the
elevational treatment.
Below: Aerial view of the new development.

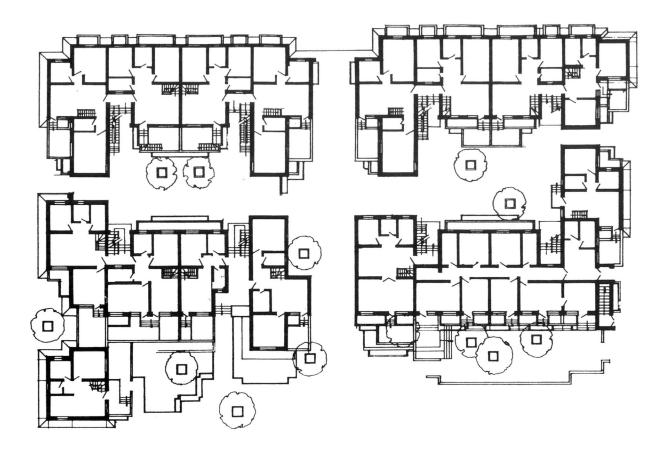

Plans of a typical cluster of units.

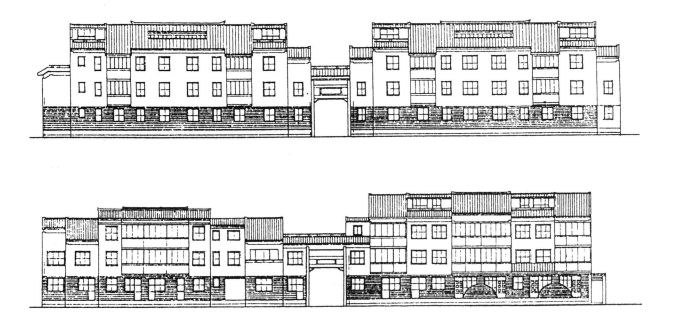

Elevations.

An intricate mix of unit types produces a complex elevation.

A strategy of organic renewal was adopted for this project which will eventually cover an area of 8.2 hectares. Well preserved buildings were retained, while others were rebuilt or repaired. Dilapidated dwellings were replaced by new courtyard houses designed in the traditional pattern.

This experimental housing project is a search for a new courtyard prototype that combines modern requirements with respect for the old fabric, while simultaneously achieving a high density development. This has been admirably fulfilled through the design which demonstrates that, given the two-and three-storey height limits, the new courtyard housing design can achieve the same density as high-rise housing. The sense of a cohesive community as well as a green and peaceful environment can also be maintained.

Details are carefully worked into the scheme in order to maximise ventilation and natural lighting. Materials used are simple, while an appropriate technology is adopted. The design has also carefully sited the blocks around existing trees, using them as a focus in the new courtyards. Under the burden of a weighty architectural heritage, the Ju'er Hutong experiment in housing has shown an optimistic and innovative way of dealing with the past.

It comes as no surprise that this project has won several state, national as well as international awards, which include the First Prize in 1993 for the Best Architecture, (awarded by the China Architectural Society); the Gold Medal for Architectural Excellence in 1992, (from the Architects Regional Council, Asia) and the World Habitat Award in 1992 from the United Nations' Building and Social Housing Foundation.

An earnest attempt is made at reducing the scale of the development.

REUTER HOUSE

SINGAPORE. 1990

WILLIAM LIM ASSOCIATES, SINGAPORE

View of the house from the entrance gate.

Completed in 1990, this house at Ridout Road in Singapore was designed by William Lim Associates. It is an important building in the oeuvre of the practice, for not only does it consolidate many earlier attempts at extending traditional imagery, but it has also become a major precedent for many subsequent works by other local practices.

Arising pragmatically from brief and site, the house's sources of inspiration derive partly from the "black-and-white bungalows" built by the British during Singapore's colonial days. Basically, the house is made up of three carefully composed blocks – an imposing two-level front block capped with a hipped roof; a linear rear block overlooking a swimming pool; and a service block that houses the kitchen, the servants' quarters and the back yard. The front block houses the more public areas of the house while the rear block is the private family domain. Natural finishes of fair-faced bricks and wide overhanging eaves lend the house its intended association with colonial bungalows.

Red *balau* timber columns left in their natural, unpainted state further contribute to the sense of formality. The roof and columns are independent of the inner concrete structure, so the roof functions like a parasol hovering over the living areas. Internal walls, floor slabs and the staircase are expressed as separate elements. The living room is contained within a light timber frame, where the sense of transparency greatly enhances the experiential aspects.

The design of this block is probably the house's most ingenious move. In a simple stroke, its Modernist sensibility demonstrates that it can be adapted to a local idiom in a new creative manner. The liberating potential offered is tremendous.

The deliberate use of contemporary materials like steel balustrades and black-painted steel capitals at the top of the timber columns set up an interesting tension with timber and other traditional materials. Horizontal timber louvres, designed to act as sunshading screens, are held between the *balau* columns. They are not really integrated into the overall design language, but there is obvious rigour in the way all the elements have been dynamically juxtaposed. The shifting of axes and skewed grids on plan further contribute a tension to the reading of the architecture.

The building is an exercise in the continuity of the spirit of the "black-and-white" colonial bungalows.

The modernist expression of concrete slabs and beams is juxtaposed with the rustic textures of timber elements.

Right: The front block of the house has a pyramidal roof supported on two-storey high timber columns.
Below: Detailed junction of the roof structure and its supporting columns.

This is an approach that is inventive, adaptive and responsive. Structure has informed space, while construction informs details. New interpretations of function have been fitted into forms which are still accessible. The house generates a great sense of place. In accommodating a modern lifestyle and exploiting local technology and materials, William Lim Associates has crafted a residence that is a potent statement of urban domesticity.

STAGE IN THE FOREST

MIYAGI, JAPAN. 1996

KENGO KUMA, JAPAN

Located in Toyama, Miyagi Prefecture, this exquisite Noh Stage was designed by Kengo Kuma & Associates. Completed in May 1996, the 550 square-metre building was conceived in such a way as to return the Noh Theatre to the natural environment in which it was traditionally performed.

Noh was originally performed in an outdoor environment, where both actors and audience had a direct contact with nature. Roofed stages were erected in natural settings. Such structures are important because the shadows cast by the roofs form part of the total experience of the theatre. However, during the Meiji era, Noh stages began to be incorporated as part of a building. This marks the evolution of *Nohgakudo*, structures which were dedicated to Noh performances. They soon sprang up all over the country, becoming part of the urban fabric. Designed as a "dumb-box", the *Nohgakudo* became less accessible to the public, and the art of watching a Noh performance in the outdoors gradually disappeared.

Kengo Kuma's long-awaited dream of recovering this important aspect of Noh theatre was fulfilled when he was commissioned to design such a building. The town of Toyama in Miyagi Prefecture is renowned for

Finely detailed timber screens create a sense of translucency, evoking an ethereal effect.

Overleaf: The emphatic linearity and planar qualities of the scheme highlight the elegant manner in which Modernism is fused with traditional forms and construction techniques.

The building is imbued with an almost surreal quality at night.

"Toyama Noh" – a tradition that dates from the Edo period. Only two places in the whole of Japan – Toyama and Kurokawa – practice this particular Noh tradition, but Toyama has always lacked a proper place for the performance of Noh.

A 1,700-square metre site in a forest on the northern edge of Toyama was chosen for the "Stage in the Forest". Kengo Kuma capitalised on the verdant beauty of the beguiling setting while impinging on it discreetly. He organised the layout with great subtlety to utilise the terrain and to exploit views, creating a stage to open out to the forest. This is an exercise in refined elementality. The *shirasu*, the gravel-paved space that traditionally surrounded the stage, was re-interpreted as an amphitheatre which serves as a landscape feature when the stage is not in use. The space beneath the stage accommodates a Noh museum in which traditional Noh costumes are displayed. The museum also serves as an evening rehearsal space for local residents.

In designing this Noh stage Kengo Kuma has set up a contrapuntal relationship between the outside and the inside. The emphatic linearity of the layout is subtly organised to utilise the terrain and to exploit views. The seating area in front of the stage – the *shomenkensho* – is designed as a transparent space with tatami flooring. During a performance, the glass partitions are removed and the space acts as a frame through which the forest as well as the Noh performance can be appreciated. This space is also used daily by the local residents in which to practice the tea ceremony and the Nihon Buto dance.

Drawing on the country's affiliation for timber, Kengo Kuma has used a light wooden latticework for the wall which separates the stage from the town. This elegant gesture creates an interface between the silent magnificence of the forest and the urban environment. Altogether, three different structural systems are used – cedar wood for the stage wing, steel frames for the seating area and reinforced concrete in the exhibition wing. Although the stage appears to follow traditional precedents, details have been abstracted and re-interpreted in a new idiom. The surface of the stage is expressed as a thin plane, possibly the first of its kind in Japan.

The "Stage in the Forest" is an exquisite building of delicate refinement replete with Japanese resonances. Kengo Kuma has created a place which combines intense reverie with sublime vitality. The highly distilled quality of the building is reminiscent of Noh theatre itself.

Thin crisp planes, like the floors and roofs, are juxtaposed with traditional roof forms in a delightful mix.

The complex impinges discreetly on its forest setting.

THE LEGIAN

BALI, INDONESIA. 1997

GRAHACIPTA HADIPRANA, INDONESIA

Designed by Indonesian architect Dedi Kusnadi of Grahacipta Hadiprana, a Jakarta-based multi-disciplinary practice, the Legian is an interesting addition to Bali's resort scene. Located in Petitenget, Legian, the hotel is probably one of the few hotels in Bali that is located as close as it is to the beach. This greatly enhances the visual and auditory links to the incessant waves.

The Legian is a relatively small and compact all-suites hotel. It has 73 one- bedroom or two-bedrooms suites. The interiors are spacious and well detailed. Due to the narrow depth of the relatively small site, the building is dispersed along the entire length of the 1.8 hectares plot of land. The four-storeyed building is almost symmetrical in plan. The centre of reflection is the entry axis, which leads from the small porte cochere into the reception lobby, continues into the restaurant, and terminates in a rectangular pool facing the sea.

Architecturally, the building draws much inspiration from traditional forms. Although not based on a transposition of specific forms, the Balinese idiom remains obvious. One senses that there is a conscious attempt in the design to depart from the trappings of traditional elements. At the same time, nonetheless, the overwhelm-

Top: A close-up of the porte cochere's multi-tiered roof.
Above left: An open-sided pavilion surrounded by a landscaped pool.
Right: A stepped walkway between two blocks leads to the beach.

ing burden of building in the Balinese context proves ponderous. For instance, the design of the porte cochere demonstrates a keen desire to imbue the building with a Modernist touch through the use of a "permeable" pyramidal structure that evokes the traditional roof form.

The Legian has also been compared with its adjacent neighbour, the fabled Oberoi Bali. Designed by Australian architect Peter Muller, the Oberoi is the forebear of many hotels in Bali. It spreads over a large tract of land, with guest accommodation consisting of single-storeyed villas nestling within lush gardens. The Legian, on the other hand, is quite a different type of hotel. Because of its tight site, The Legian generates the feel of a city hotel. Its imposing structure may not exactly earn accolades, but it is certainly interesting as it differs from many other resorts in Bali.

However, one should not fixate on the Balinese elements alone. There is a clear expressiveness in the use of architectural elements. Spaces are handled with a light touch. The desire to achieve simplicity is evident. Low ceiling spaces at the ground level, for example, imbue the place with a particular intimacy. It is a neat orchestration of sensitive planning and a controlled use of materials.

Detailing is straightforward and simplified, while a muted colour palette is used throughout the building. Walkways linking the public spaces are successfully treated in this respect. They extend the sense of space quite successfully, and also enable one to move effortlessly between indoors and outdoors. Landscaping details, such as the use of large bodies of reflecting pools between the guest room blocks, help to make the whole complex appear much larger than it actually is.

In the interiors, Indonesian interior designer Jaya Ibrahim has created a sense of asceticism through the subtle play of light and muted colours. Pared details contribute to the building's serene repose. A contemplative quiescence pervades the spaces. At night, the lights create a thoroughly subdued ambiance that greatly enhance the introspective, low-key mood. It is truly a santuary of uninvaded calm.

Ibrahim has crafted a cool guest room interior. His lightness of touch is deftly executed. The colour palette is limited to whites and browns. Refined finishes add a touch of luxury. Bathrooms are designed as sybaritic havens. All the various pieces of loose furniture come together in a coherent whole. Constructed with simple lines and using local materials, they exude an overall sense of quiet dignity. Treading a fine line between the kind of minimalist trend so pervasive these days and the elaborate ornamentation of traditional Indonesian furniture, Ibrahim has crafted a delightful interior that possesses a pervasive sensuality and understated elegance which thrills the senses.

The Legian joins the growing rank of designs in Asia which seek out continuities with local traditions. These projects evoke or quote directly and indirectly from forms and features of past sources. So long as an attempt at internalising them is made, this particularisation of accepted idioms should be welcomed.

Top: Colonnaded walkways accentuate the perception of depth.
Right: Reflecting pools are located in the courtyards between the various blocks.

Overleaf: At night, the architectural details and lighting effects combine to produce a serene composition of horizontal and vertical lines.

WAT PA SUNANTHAWANARAM

KANCHANABURI, THAILAND. 1996

NITHI STHAPITANONDA, ARCHITECTS 49

One usually envisages Thai Buddhist temples, or *wat*, as huge complexes inlaid with glittering ornaments and shimmering tiles. Wat Pa Sunanthawanaram, designed by Nithi Sthapitanonda of Architects 49, is the exact antithesis of such imagery.

As hubs for spiritual and social life, Buddhist temples, created by ancient kings as symbols of their omnipotence, are believed to be representations of the universal cosmology. Their architectural manifestations often assume the grandeur deemed appropriate for such a building type.

However, Wat Pa Sunathawanaram veers away from this typology in its form, materials and expression. Located in Kanchanaburi province, the temple is affiliated with the famous Wat Nong Pa Phong, where simplicity is a way of life. A sense of asceticism extends to every detail of Wat Pa Sunathawanaram. The architecture distills the essentials, and eradicates the ubiquitous ornamentation found in traditional Thai temples.

The temple differs from traditional Thai temples in its simplicity and absence of ornamentation.

Right: A bamboo trellis casts a fine texture of shadows on the columns.

The main Buddha image is placed outside the hall, facing east.

The temple's multi-purpose hall is a single storeyed structure inspired by the vernacular architecture of the region. It comprises a main practice hall and two wings of semi-open rooms for praying. These structures enclose an open courtyard which is used primarily for meditation.

A deft manipulation of materials has resulted in a building which is full of understated charm. Materials, which are left in their natural states, are used for their textures and finishes. Floors are finished with polished concrete. In the prayer rooms, the floors are raised and finished in used timber. The main Buddha image is placed, facing east, outside the hall. A bamboo trellis filters light onto the image, casting a subdued glow that serves to make the image the visual focus. The grandeur of the richly nuanced space is impressive.

Overall, the minimalist quality of the temple design causes it to project an aura of humility. Composed with vigour and skill, the temple is a sanctuary of absolute calm. Perceived as manifesting an "architecture of wisdom", the temple is intended as a haven in which devotees can seek "truth" and "enlightenment". It is a delightful result of the architect's scrupulousness and confident configuration of space and materials. The disciplined restraint with which the whole has been articulated and detailed has resulted in an eloquent piece of work.

Use of simple materials has resulted in a building full of understand charm.

CHAPTER 7

REINTERPRETING TRADITION
THE USE OF CONTEMPORARY IDIOMS

For many architects, a return to the kind of tradition of the pre-Industrial era is unthinkable. Theirs is an approach which does not accept that there is a fixed and immutable relation between form and meaning. It tries to understand the traditional typology and attempts to modify the representational systems it has inherited. Based on the difficult attempt to recover the deeper layers of the architectural tradition through fundamentals abstracted from the past, such an approach aims for a new critical awareness and a reinterpretation of the meaning which belongs to the particular tradition.

Sentimental recovery of the past is jettisoned while histrionic gestures are abandoned. Instead, an invigorating modern idiom is used. Nevertheless, the build-

"We can use the past fruitfully only when we realise that to inherit is also to transform. What our predecessors have left us deserves respect, but a patrimony simply preserved becomes an intolerable burden; the past is best used by being domesticated – and by our accepting and rejoicing that we do so."

– David Lowenthal, *The Past is a Foreign Country*.

ings created through this approach are dedicated to place and history without being trapped by the latter. Traditional formal devices are not discarded but are transformed in refreshing ways. There is a simultaneous acknowledgment of the past and the present through an abstract and usually minimalist statement.

In many ways, Frampton's attempt at returning architecture's basis to the idea of the "tectonic" is reflected in many of these schemes. Throughout history, the best works have always combined a sense of tradition with a keen awareness of their own contemporaneity. One needs only to look at Frank Lloyd Wright's transformation of Meso-American forms or Luis Barragan's use of Mexico's Hispanic past and deep cultural roots to see

this approach exemplifed.

It is significant that most of the works in this category share a common laconic quality. Perhaps this is a reflection of current international trends as well. Juries of recent prestigious awards, in their citations, inevitably lament the incessant search for the novel. A perceptible trend has now emerged where less is taken to be definitely more. This wave of minimalist works suffers the risk of coalescing into yet another stylistic approach.

Juhani Pallasmaa poses what he considers one of the essential questions of the architectural profession today: *"Can architecture re-create a tradition, a shared ground which provides a basis for the criteria of authenticity and quality?"* [1]

One of the six themes Pallasmaa suggests for the

re-enchantment of architecture at the the turn of the millennium includes *"Authenticity"*, which he defines *"more as the quality of deep rootedness in the stratifications of culture."* He further argues that *"as our existential experience loses its coherence through the mosaic of placeless and timeless information, we become detached from traditional sources of identity ... Authenticity of architectural works supports a confidence in time and human nature; it provides the ground for individual identity."* [2]

1. Juhani Pallasmaa. 1994. "Six Themes For The Next Millenium" in the *Architectural Review*, July, p.76.
2. Ibid.

JAYAKODY HOUSE

COLOMBO, SRI LANKA. 1994

GEOFFREY BAWA, SRI LANKA

The entrance court is a simple synthesis of stark planar walls.

In this urban house located in the inner suburbs of central Colombo, Geoffrey Bawa has designed an interesting structure that on first impression appears to be a departure from his repertoire of formal vocabulary and his accustomed palette. Presenting an appropriately demure front to the street, the house's reticent and understated elevation belies a rich interior.

Sited on an awkward plot of land, the house turns inwards and focuses on two triangular courtyards. The effect creates a series of alternating interior and exterior spaces that coalesce into a single harmonious entity.

The sequence of movement through the various spaces has been superbly orchestrated. An open-air entry court leads into an intimate entrance hall. This is directly linked to the living room and the dining room. Both spaces overlook two private courtyards with different coloured walls. The visual contrast sets up an interesting juxta-position of different moods. A huge jar located at the end of the dining room is lit from above by natural light. The scale of the jar, set against a backdrop of planes painted in blue hues, is visually quite spectacular. Furniture is deployed sparingly, but to great effect.

View of the severe elevations. The external staircase leading to the roof terrace is enclosed by a decorative metal cage.

The second storey houses the bedrooms, while the third storey provides an open terrace, a guest bedroom and an informal living space. Two rooftop terraces provide excellent vantage points from which to look across the parks and gardens in the city.

Though designed with a severe Modernist restraint, the Jayakody house is anchored in Sri Lanka's traditional architectural lessons. The seamless interface with the external environment is particularly noteworthy. It refreshingly addresses the role that courtyards can physically play, as well as their phenomenological presence within a building in the tropical context. In combining vernacular lessons with a humanistic interpretation of modernism, the house also shares a trajectory quite similar to the oeuvre of Luis Barragan's later works – where the abstract deployment of planes and sunwashed colours is primarily concerned with the poetics of architecture.

This house demonstrates, in the most poetic manner possible, that simple pleasures of light, space and materials have a lyrical power to move the inner self. Above all, it succinctly illustrates Bawa's deeply felt conviction that the critical component of architecture is the life it accommodates.

Left: A huge earthern jar is spectacularly lit by natural light filtering down an internal court.

Above: The dining space overlooks the internal court and the outdoor courtyard.

Above: Exquisite pieces of furniture contribute to the overall
sense of contemplative silence.

Left: View of the outdoor courtyard from the living space.

From the living space, the visitor has views of all the three courtyards.

MURASAKINO WAKUDEN

KYOTO, JAPAN. 1995

WARO KISHI, JAPAN

The intimate reception area is designed in an understated tone.

The works of Japanese architect Waro Kishi are noteworthy for sensitively evoking the local nuance through appropriating the language of architectural modernity. His unique sense of asceticism and cultured discipline have won him numerous awards, including the Japan Institute of Architects Award for the best young architect of the year in 1991.

Kishi's pursuit of architecturally engaging functionalism infused with the essence of "Japaneseness" is evident in one of his most recent works, a Japanese restaurant in Kyoto. An intimately small commission, the Restaurant Wakuden is essentially an *Obento Ya* ("a lunch-box shop") inserted into a 70 square-metre plot of land. It is a box-like, three-storeyed structure that appears effacingly simple. Located at the end of a row of bland townhouses, the structure's reticence allows it to sit comfortably within its context.

However, the boldness of the simple gesture, where a three-storeyed timber screen is flanked by bare concrete walls, ensures that the building brandishes its presence, albeit in a subtle manner. This internalised treatment shields the restaurant from the noise of Kitaoji Avenue, one of the main thoroughfares of Kyoto.

A large timber screen presents an inscrutable and uncompromising front to the busy street.

Programmatically, the design starts from general principles using a reductionist palette. The first storey consists of a reception and sales area for take-away lunch boxes. The second storey houses the main dining hall, while the third storey contains the kitchen and service areas. A small garden is carved out of the small space within the first storey, allowing light and the presence of nature to filter into the interiors. The enclosed nature of this ground floor exudes a great sense of serenity, while the second storey opens out to the west through a fine timber louvred screen. Views are directed towards the verdant greenery of the Daitokuji temple complex on the opposite side.

Filled with light, Kishi's luminous space evokes qualities associated with traditional Japanese architecture in which, historically, timber was one of the principal materials used. Kishi uses it in a new and refreshing manner. The timber screen brings in filtered light, producing an effect similar to that of the traditional Japanese sliding screens. At the same time, the Japanese notion of borrowed landscape is expressed in the way the architect directs the views from within the building. The roof is a gently pitched structure, thus allowing the building to blend into its context when seen from a higher vantage point. However, this pitch is not visible at road level. Instead, an I-beam running along the fascia produces a "floating edge" effect, imbuing it with a pronounced sense of horizontality.

Kishi has consciously sought to express *Wafu*, the Japanese sense of style, through the use of a modern vocabulary, which in this case is essentially reinforced concrete. Committed as much to modernity as to Japanese culture, he utilises a reductionist palette, where details are understated and simple materials are used to achieve maximum effects. This is reflected in the fine attention lavished on details as well as the care and thought that have been spent on the creation of an intensely tactile architecture. It is a commanding piece of crafted artifice, one where the past is framed in terms of its significance for today.

A reductionist palette is evident in the treatment of interior spaces.

Below: The finely detailed timber screen is a reinterpretation of the
traditional *shoji* screen.

Right: The gently pitched roof is not visible from the road level. Instead,
an I-beam running along the fascia produces a "floating edge" effect.
Overleaf: The focus of the small restaurant's interior is a courtyard at the end
of the room.

AKENO VILLAGE SOLAR BATH HOUSES

TOKYO, JAPAN. 1991

YOSHIO KATO, JAPAN

Careful considerations of the building's orientation and placement of openings have resulted in comfortable interior spaces.

As we enter the next millennium, the key issue for architecture is not about style, but of addressing the problems of damage to the world environment and the depletion of its natural resources. We have recently been warned yet again – by the International Panel on Climate Change (IPCC), a respected UN-sponsored body – of the reality of global warming. New evidence indicates that the emissions of heat-trapping gases could drive global temperatures up as much as 4° C by the year 2100 AD.

There can be no doubt that a more sensible use of energy in buildings would effect a major alteration in carbon dioxide production. It is estimated that 60 per cent of total carbon dioxide emissions are produced by building and construction industries alone. In recognising this factor, architects cannot continue to practice in defiance of nature. There is a ground swell of real concern about ecological issues. Renewable materials, energy conservation and green buildings are the keywords used by every architect who wants to be taken seriously. However, there are still relatively few built models that can serve as exemplars in this direction.

The cost savings of constructing new buildings which use energy efficiently are quite clear. By maximisng the

The bath house is inspired by forms from vernacular designs.

use of ambient energy and passive solar energy strategies, the need for artificial cooling, lighting and ventilation can be greatly reduced.

One designer who has been actively pursuing the practice of energy-efficient, passive solar building design for the last 15 years is Japanese architect Yoshio Kato. Working in Tokyo, Kato has designed many exquisite small houses that demonstrate interesting advances in using ambient energy, based on knowledge gained from the study of traditional dwellings.

These inventive built examples include the use of active and passive solar collectors, solar chimneys and thermal walls. A pair of solar bath houses designed by Kato in Japan exemplifies many of the strategies he uses in his works.

The first bath house is designed for members of an amusement park development. Situated in the mountainous suburbs of Tokyo, at 1,000 m above sea level, it was constructed in 1991. Passive solar methods in this bath house include "sun rooms" with glass walls, earth berms and rock beds. The water in the solar tubes in the sun room is heated by direct solar heat gain and re-heated to provide hot water for the bathrooms. Warm air from the rock beds beneath the floor of the sun room is also circulated to other areas through tubes laid underground. The comfortable interior is finished in local wood sourced from the nearby mountains. A careful consideration of the orientation and placement of openings has resulted in rich interior spaces that are modest but effective.

Another house utilises the same systems as this bath house, as well as active solar water collectors on its roof. Kato's responsive synthesis of modern technology and traditional knowledge is a remarkable example of how best to respond to the challenge of sustainability with creative design solutions and energy efficient strategies. His houses demonstrate how architecture can take cues from indigenous archetypes, and work in concert with the natural environment through strategies from site orientation to an enlightened use of energy and efficient ventilation systems.

Kato's brave moves are the exception rather than the rule in current architecture. Nonetheless, they offer grounds for optimism. If the vision of a sustainable future is to be realised, attitudes must change, and energy efficient designs vigorously pursued in a truly collective manner.

The roof is a key component of the energy-efficient design.

Right: Traditional methods of construction
are employed in the design of the roof.

BUMI ASAH

PUNCAK, INDONESIA. 1996

GRAHACIPTA HADIPRANA, INDONESIA

A traditional Balinese rice barn serves as a garden pavilion.

Hovering above a pool of water, Bumi Asah is a simple and unassuming timber pavilion with an all-encompassing tranquillity. Shrouded in mist and surrounded by towering pines, it is hard to imagine that this structure, with its prosaic elegance, is located only one-and-a-half hours away from Jakarta, the capital of Indonesia.

Situated in the cool highlands of Puncak (which literally means "the summit"), this pavilion is part of an assembly of four structures designed by Indonesian architect Sindhu Hadiprana. Completed towards the end of 1996, the complex is used for the training of staff, as well as for seminars and brain-storming sessions for Hadiprana's office and other corporate organisations.

This cluster of timber structures succeeds in embodying a certain stillness, and proffers lessons for the design of serene environments. It makes an explicit connection with nature, evoking a direct and emotive relationship with the verdant landscape.

The complex is known as Bumi Asah, which is a combination of two Indonesian terms – *Bumi*, which means "the making of the earth" and *Asah*, which means "the cultivation of common goals". The name thus symbolises the idea of team work as the foundation for quality.

Bare concrete walls and timber furniture create a tranquil interior setting.

Throughout, Hadiprana has infused the space with his personal collection of traditional artifacts which are associated with the notion of team work. Symbols, both abstract and literal, are used in abundance. These symbols are all related to the concept of synergy and knowledge. The conceptual basis for the design is also unique in that the architect chose to combine some of the management principles suggested in Diane Tracy's best-seller, *10 Steps to Empowerment*, with Javanese and Balinese concepts of team work.

Compositionally, four pavilions are organised in an open configuration that emphasises an overlapping of views. They are linked by two simple, open-sided corridors. A statue of Ganesha, symbolising "education and knowledge", is placed at the entrance lobby. It was made by the Balinese sculptor Sdr. Winten. The positioning of the statute is also located within a space flanked by the original door panels of a Balinese rice storage barn, to symbolise the storage of knowledge.

The entrance pavilion, also known as the Synergy Room, is a simple 8-metre square structure. Mounted on the ceiling is a dedeleg, a decorative ceiling panel which is normally used as an important element in a traditional Balinese house. This panel consists of five elements, each of which was carved separately by different artists. The process symbolises the concept of *"gotong royong"*, which is the Indonesian and Malay for team work. Installed as a unified piece, the dedeleg is used as an important example of synergised team work. The exquisite table located in the middle of the room is a batik-producing instrument. Again, the production of batik is associated with a group of people working in harmony.

The entrance pavilion leads into the Conference Room, which is actually the pivot of the entire architectural setting. Supported by stilts and cantilevered over a pool of water, there is a pervading sense of lightness throughout the whole space. The quality of ever-changing light reflected off the water is especially magical at night.

View of the conference block from the dining room.

A huge wooden carving of an ancient boat (another symbol of team work) forms the support for a long conference table. The edge of the floor is finished with 19mm thick glass sheets which allow the occupants to enjoy the visual delight of moving water beneath the floor. Bold displays of foliage are also carefully framed as part of the views from the room.

Open transitions between the various rooms abet interaction. An open-sided corridor links the Entrance Pavilion and the Conference Room to a Multi-Purpose Room on one side and a Guest Lodge on the other. The Multi-Purpose Room is used for dining and for informal discussions. Overlooking a lawn on which nine pine trees have been planted, this room offers immediate and direct contact with the landscape. The ambiguous relationship between inside and outside is exploited to provide a general feeling of great repose. Spatially, the Multi-Purpose Room is executed with rigorous intensity. Openings are designed in an unaffected manner. Un-plastered walls and rough-hewn timber supports are all part of the understated vocabulary.

The design of Bumi Asah is very much a personal commentary. Hadiprana believes in the design of build-

ings dedicated to place and history without being trapped by the latter. Although the design is loaded with traditional symbols, the complex is a harmonious convergence of the old and the new. All the columns, to take one example, are made of recycled timber poles that were used since the 1920s to carry electrical cables in Bali. Their raw texture embodies a unique elemental quality.

More importantly, Bumi Asah celebrates the joy of tropical living through its fluid interaction between outdoor and indoor spaces, steeply pitched roofs with wide overhanging eaves, and its concern for shade and cross ventilation. It surprises guests at every junction with palpable qualities of materiality and a real sense of place. The interweaving of building, site and culture offers evidence that an invigorating reinterpretation of traditional lessons can produce a pleasurable yet relevant contemporary architecture.

170 BUKIT TIMAH ROAD

SINGAPORE. 1997

KERRY HILL ARCHITECTS, SINGAPORE

A balau timber screen acts as a filter between the internal and external environments.

This mixed-use development by Kerry Hill Architects marks an important point of departure in the practice's oeuvre. Perceived by many as being strictly resort designers, in this building on Bukit Timah Road Kerry Hill Architects demonstrate their ability to produce other building types that carry the same conviction and clarity as their resorts have done.

Completed in mid-1997, this building exemplifies the beliefs of the practice, and its principals – in particular, Kerry Hill – concerning both the materiality of architecture and the transformation of tradition. Known as "Genesis", the building replaces four shophouses, which, in Singapore, are a traditional form of terraced housing-cum-place of work. In his 1822 *Town Plan of Singapore*, Stamford Raffles had allowed for a linear arrangement of shophouses of specified widths linked by a five-foot wide colonnaded walkway, which came to be known as the "five-foot-way". Traders conducted their trade on the ground level and lived in small rooms on the upper one or two floors. Subsequently, in response to the needs of the local populace, the built-form that emerged from Raffles's 1822 Town Plan became a dominant urban typology that characterised

Right: The front facade faces the busy Bukit Timah Road.

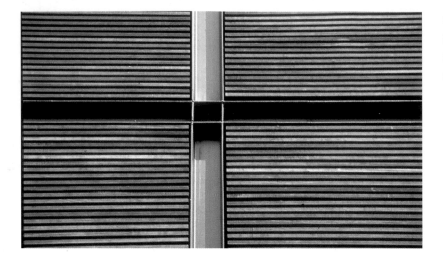

most of the towns of British Southeast Asia.

The new development is located along a busy stretch of road at Bukit Timah. In replacing existing shophouses, Genesis draws extensively on their architectural lessons. Traditional elements such as louvred windows and internal courtyards have been re-interpreted and transformed into a contemporary building of great verve. The projects of Kerry Hill Architects exhibit a tendency towards designing from general principles, using a reductionist palette. This reductionist tendency should not be confused with the oft-quoted "Less is More" stylistic idiom that appears to be sweeping the international scene at the moment. Rather, a project like Genesis should be evaluated in terms of its ability to craft "more with less".

The finely honed building houses four apartments above two floors of office space and a showroom, forming, in effect, a contemporary version of the shophouse. The colour of the external walls is mustard, while that of the service cores is grey. The interior is painted in a stark white. These three colours come together on adjacent walls in the internal light well, and together with a black reflecting pool, form an abstract composition.

Lightweight, semi-permeable walls have always been

a feature of buildings in this part of the world. Their role is to maximise the interface between the internal space and the surroundings. Instead of excluding the weather and isolating the building's occupants from the external environment, the architecture filters the outside selectively through a system of louvred openings. The building, which is only 16 metres deep, thus offers immediate and direct contact with the environment.

In this astutely crafted project, the ability to respond perceptively to tradition while using contemporary technology is exemplary. It combines the lessons of traditional louvred windows with the desire for a lightness of expression to create a simple box whose *parti* is simply a finely detailed timber screen across the facade of the building.

Finely detailed, the *balau* timber louvres can be adjusted by a motorised control system. This is a sophisticated re-interpretation of an old ventilation technique. The system ingeniously combines a device found in shophouses built during the colonial period with lessons from contemporary technology to form an effective urban landmark. It is a bold building that provides a new way of looking at the world.

Interesting play of colours on adjacent walls in the internal light well.

Above: Filtered light creates an interesting texture of shadows on the walls of the fourth and fifth storey apartments.

Right: A timber-decked verandah acts as a transition zone between the privacy of the apartment and the public front of the timber screen.

THE SERAI

BALI, INDONESIA. 1994

KERRY HILL ARCHITECTS, SINGAPORE

Located on the east coast of Bali, The Serai is only a short distance from Candi Desa, an outpost of rural charm and beautiful beaches. The resort is designed for the budget traveler and consists of 56 standard guest rooms and two suites, all of which are accommodated within four separate two-storeyed blocks with sweeping vistas across the swimming pool to the beach.

This is an interesting experiment in creating a new niche market, in which architecture becomes an important marketing tool. Although the result is far from reductionist, the reductionist palette of the architect is evident, with the formal moves being deliberately safe. On first impression, the most striking aspect of the building is that it appears simple and rather reticent, almost too minimal in its details. But it soon became apparent that this is a welcome virtue.

An appreciation of the careful choice of materials and the articulation of joints is made much more easy because of the economy of means. The detailing is everywhere very understated, and demonstrates an impressive ability to make the few and relatively cheap materials achieve maximum effects. Lavish attention is spent on subtle details that dignify simple construction.

150 | 151

Above: The enormous reception lobby is designed
in the simplest of styles.
Right: View of the restaurant block from the lobby.

Site plan showing the positioning of the guest
room blocks around the swimming pool.

The architectural language is developed through
the exploitation of constructional logic and close considerations of use and site conditions. The carefully proportioned and articulated blocks are set facing the
main swimming pool. In the compositional sense, each
block is immutably related to the surrounding environment as well as to each other. There is an overall
languorous quality about the entire composition. The
orthogonal planning grid is skewed against the beach
line to maximise ocean views, and the buildings are dispersed along the perimeter of the site in order to display
the coconut grove.

Although the construction of the building makes
use of site-specific natural materials such as coconut
wood, ochre coloured stones, bamboo and teak wood,
it manages to transcend the Balinese imagery that has
become so much like a formula in many hotel designs
on the island.

Guest rooms are entered in pairs from a detached
open walkway positioned at mid level between floors.
Wide overhanging eaves contribute to the pronounced
horitzontality that creates a close relationship to the
ground. Carefully constructed views also offer surprises
at various points along the promenade.

The design is an example of a contemplative sort
of architecture that seems so unselfconscious in its
effects. Without mimicking the traditional Balinese
forms or descending into kitsch, the architect uses an
abstract and austere vocabulary to evoke the local
nuance. The outcome seems so uncontrived that it has
a sense of inevitability.

Detail of a water channel in the
landscaped pool.

The guest room blocks are oriented towards the pool and the sea.

Overleaf: Clean, uncluttered lines make a potent architectural statement.

Above: Steps at the junction between two guest room blocks.

Right: The entrance path to the ground floor guest rooms is built on a landscaped moat.

Left: Guest rooms on different levels are given contrasting treatment.

RIMBUN DAHLAN

KUANG, MALAYSIA. 1996

HIJAS KASTURI, MALAYSIA

Set in an open, park-like environment,
the house is a place of contemplation.

Removed from the bustle of Kuala Lumpur, this house is a tranquil retreat that combines a certain serenity with vivacity. Through adroit architectural sleights of hand, architect Hijas Kasturi has managed to infuse this house, which serves as his own residence, with an opportunistic use of materials as well as his characteristic ebullience

While Kasturi celebrates indigenous architecture, the result is not mere imitation. He has added a new level of excitement not found in traditional structures. Located at the 27 km mark on Jalan Kuang in Kuang, Selangor, the house is sited within a large 14-acre plot of land. Designed with a mix of concrete columns and steel trusses instead of timber, basically the house takes the traditional Malaysian form and reinterprets it, using a contemporary idiom. Architectural elements associated with *kampung* houses (village houses) are all there – broad sloping roofs, natural ventilation, concealed grilles instead of glass, and the use of local materials. An oxidised copper roof replaces the traditional thatch or *attap*.

A distinctive hallmark of the house is the generosity of the spaces, each of which is treated in a dramatic way. The guest house and studios are separated from the

Right: View of the main house and the guest house.

The linkway has wonderful views of the vast grounds.

main house. The studio space below the guest rooms is intended as a work space for resident artists. Their independent access ensures privacy for the occupants. A covered linkway, which overlooks a large reflective pool and a cascade, joins the main house and guest house. This space serves as a huge dining area when necessary. The garden is filled with hundreds of trees and palms, all indigenous to Southeast Asia. An adjacent herb garden will be planted with traditional medicinal plants as well as with spices, culinary herbs and vegetables.

This is an absolutely unpretentious house. Kasturi's skill in infusing eclectic past forms with robust inventions is indisputable, while his concern for details impresses. Detailed with an explicit rigour, terrazo finishes are used liberally while the beams, pillars and verandah walls are finished in Shanghai plaster – an old technique in which granite chips are bonded in a rough texture, then applied over the surfaces.

The house is imposing, yet somehow ephemeral. Confident in its manner of interweaving formal themes with the variants of circulation and experiential richness, the house has a certain lyricism and grace not often found in traditional architecture.

Kasturi's works evince the successful integration and combination of the prosaic with the poetic. Like most of his earlier works, the house is inspired by such features as the climate, the quality of the local light, structural expression, topography, materials and craft. The boldly expressive design especially manipulates light and materials in a new dynamic synthesis. As the owners themselves proudly declared: "This building is of its time and place, designed to nurture not just one family but several, and hopefully to encourage new attitudes to cultural development and environmental awareness." Although modest in its aspirations, it is undoubtedly a valid synthesis of Malaysian prototypes.

Above: Internal volumes are animated by roof trusses.
Right: Contemporary, sleek finishes add a touch of elegance to the interiors.

HOUSE AT CHATSWORTH PARK

SINGAPORE. 1997

WILLIAM LIM ASSOCIATES, SINGAPORE

Comprising four houses on adjacent lots, this complex is designed by William Lim Associates. One of the houses is an existing colonial bungalow that has been conserved. The architectural vocabulary of the conserved house forms the basis for the design language of the other units. Acknowledging such givens, the houses are conceived as an expression of "contemporary vernacular", where the language of the past is "modernised" in subtle ways.

These houses are oriented according to site conditions, and the overall composition is very much an intricately woven one. An existing tree was kept during the design stage, and it forms the focus for the entire composition. Although the houses are visually related through a similar material palette, each house has a different layout, and consequently, markedly different internal characters. However, each of the houses aims at achieving an integral relationship with the outdoors. The subtle gradations of space result in a diversity of outdoor and indoor realms.

The first unit of these houses encapsulates most of the prevailing design themes. It tries to evolve a viable modern language that draws upon traditional proto-

Above: Elevation of the front portico.
Right: Huge pivoting doors open out to the terrace and swimming pool at the rear of the house.

Left: The staircase leads up to the private spaces above.
Below: View of the internal atrium.

types. In its planning, the house is basically a box, with a central atrium-like space which serves as a covered courtyard. An internal fish pond completes the composition. A staircase hidden behind a feature wall terminates at the pool. This space engages on a highly visceral level. Changing levels of light throughout the day animate the entire house. Spaces revolve around this central atrium. On the upper level, a walkway fringes the void over this atrium. Voluminous spaces and the effect of filtered light evoke a great sense of quietude.

To move around the houses, either inside or outside, is to experience an interesting series of perspectives that use each of the other houses as a part of the composition. The spaces have a sensorial strength because kinetic activities are harnessed as part of the circulation route. The house itself has a unique legibility not based upon the conventional sequence of domestic design.

Lavish attention has obviously been spent on subtle details. Timber is used liberally throughout the house. In its simplicity, the house recall the traditional courtyard houses of China. Yet the details are obviously designed for a tropical environment. This house at Chatsworth Park projects an image of confident modernity while striving to achieve a sense of tropical vitality.

HOUSE AT BLAIR ROAD

SINGAPORE. 1996

RICHARD HO ARCHITECTS, SINGAPORE

The stairwell is the focus of the entire house.

Singapore architect Richard Ho has done a series of exquisite renovations to old shophouses that have been conserved. These works succinctly illustrate Ho's design philosophy as well as an evolving, but clearly eloquent materialist aesthetics.

Ho set up his practice in 1991 on his return to Singapore after several fruitful years of work experience in Austria and Italy. The young practice's overriding concern is to "use architecture as an expression of the continuity of the history of civilisation, the memory of cities and man's unending endeavour to be in harmony with his soul and the world he lives in."

This deeply felt conviction manifests itself in all the firm's projects, but is especially poignant in the way Ho deals with the renovations of several shophouses. Issues of tradition and innovation, continuity and change, conservation and adaptation, are explored and tackled through architectural moves that are both radical as well as ultimately sensible, and minimal yet highly effective.

The shophouse is a colonial legacy in Southeast Asia. Its typical features include brick walls with high ceilings, roofs with secondary jack-roofs to allow hot

Right: View of the staircase and the enclosing "box".

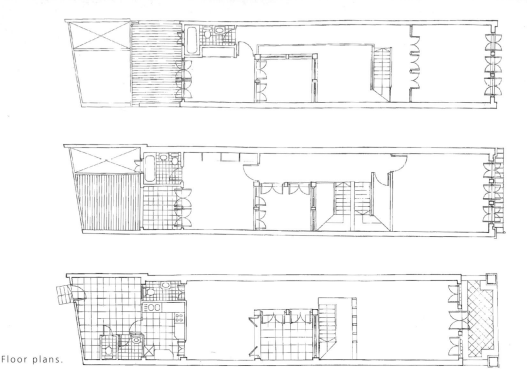

Floor plans.

air to escape, an airwell to provide light and ventilation, and a shop-front on the first storey. The early prototypes of these buildings were purely utilitarian, and only in the early 1900s were elaborate architectural motifs from European, Malay and Chinese architecture introduced to the front facades. Although the conservation and restoration of areas rich in historic architecture is essential in providing tangible links to Singapore's heritage, the allure of shophouses as an alternative housing type is probably due to their currently limited numbers. Ho re-designed a number of these shophouses, his first winning the Singapore Institute of Architects' Design Award in 1995.

The shophouses were first gutted then redesigned with a clever manipulation of planes and vertical elements, paying respect to the past in the internal ordering of space, which centres around the courtyard typology while having an integrity wholly their own. The external fabric, including the front elevation and rear extension, remains intact as part of the planning authorities' guidelines. Internally, however, the house was radically re-configured with the courtyard being accentuated. Several key ideas and enlightened strategies persist throughout the various shophouse schemes. The internal volumes become light-modulators whose focus is always a light-well. This is an important pivotal point and also the most dramatic design element, providing diffused light to the floors.

The sense of transparency is heightened through a deliberate placement of planes and lines of sight within this spatial matrix. This is especially poignant in the house at Blair Road. Spaces are layered intricately by inserting walls and openings. These become "frames" accentuating the distance between subject and object, yet enhancing the overall sense of depth.

The triumph in this shophouse lies in its discipline and total lack of contrivance – the architect doing only the essential to create an internal environment both functional and attractive. For all its simplicity and studied minimalism, the house is a delight. A rigorous attention to detail is obvious, the use of steel and glass registering a sleek contemporary touch to an otherwise predominantly timber palette. But the qualities that register most vividly are the simple pleasures of space, light and the materials – fundamentals of architecture that are all too often drowned by chaotic clutter in contemporary works. This desire to eradicate the cacophonous has been consistent throughout Ho's portfolio.

Bathed in light, the house resonates with a white brilliance.

HOUSE AT EVERTON ROAD

SINGAPORE. 1997

WILLIAM LIM ASSOCIATES, SINGAPORE

View of the central courtyard from the entrance doors.

Most of the conserved shophouses in Singapore are exercises in dexterous spatial remodeling. The play of the staircase usually constitutes the bold stroke of the *parti*. But this unit at Everton Road is quite an exception. Here, the staircases are discreetly hidden away.

Infusing rationality with the expressive potency of light and space, this is a delightful shophouse conceptualised by architect Mok Wei Wei of William Lim Associates. Blending a refreshing solution with a practical reality, this light-filled scheme has been carefully designed with a clean-cut philosophy.

The genesis of the house is in response to the inherent constraints of a shophouse. The composition of interior and exterior space, vertical and horizontal dimensions, is crafted with respect to the original sequence of space. The main architectural preoccupations of the architect are with space and light. The subtle play of light, instead of volume in this instance, asserts an air of meditative power. Several spatial moves, made within a relatively tight budget but with unflagging rigour, prove that simplicity can be both stunning and practical.

Marked by an apparent modesty, materials and detailing are essentially simple. Travertine is used at the

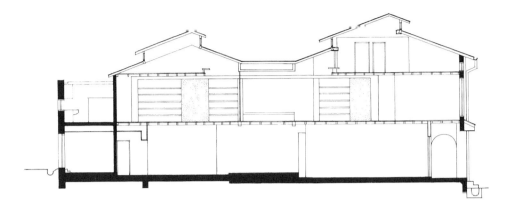

first storey while timber is used for the upper levels. The living room is located immediately behind the entrance doors. From here, the space leads to a courtyard that is framed by a simple screen. Clad in travertine, the screen's intended effect appears diminished by its hesistancy. The issue of whether it should serve as a screen or as a frame has not been clearly defined in its architectural form. The courtyard is treated simply, filled with pebbles and remnant fragments of the original granite slabs. A dining room is located adjacent to the courtyard. The kitchen and other service areas are located towards the rear.

Tucked to the side of the party wall is the staircase – a straight flight to the second floor. Here the sequence of spaces are more marked by the presence of walls enclosing the central courtyard. The presence of a generous bathroom at the rear of the house at this level acts as a visual focus. The bathroom, replete with the luxury of an outdoor jacuzzi , is subtly hidden by sliding panels. These sliding panels – consisting of frosted glass and solid panels painted white – are a recurring theme throughout the house.

Two small, loft-like spaces are accessed by separate staircases from the second storey. The house asserts an air of unadorned simplicity. Although the architect's palette is rigorously simple, there is a spirit of refined intensity. This is a house that avoids rhetorical language. It is a controlled statement using a rigorously limited palette of materials. It is significant in the way it departs from the usual practice of using the vertical circulation as an architectural focus in the design of conserved shophouses.

Above: View of the internal volumes from the attic.
Overleaf: The central courtyard is the focus of the first storey.

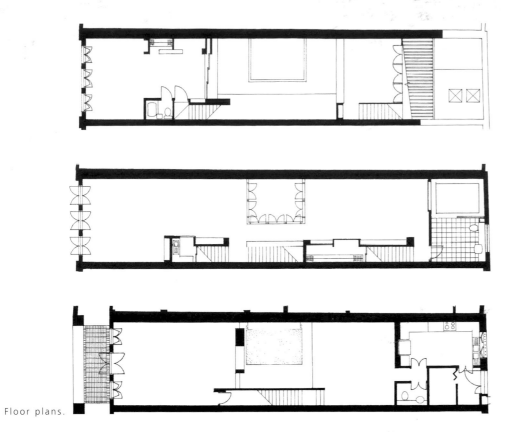

Floor plans.

White finishes throughout the house set up a light, airy ambiance. The
bathroom is enlivened by the outdoor jacuzzi.

Right: Sliding screens of frosted glass are used extensively.

PHOTO CREDITS

- Novotel Benoa
  Pictures by Tan Hock Beng and Lek Bunnag
- Teahouse
  All pictures courtesy of Feng Jizhong
- National Crafts Museum
  Pictures courtesy of Charles Correa and Robert Powell
- House at Swiss Club Road
  Pictures courtesy of B&S&T Architects
- Kandawgyi Palace Hotel
  Pictures courtesy of Lek Bunnag and Bill Bensley
- Miyagi Sant Juan Bautista Museum
  Pictures courtesy of Kazuhiro Ishii
- Jawahar Kala Kendra
  Pictures courtesy of Charles Correa and Robert Powell
- Banyan Tree Maldives
  Pictures courtesy of Banyan Tree Resorts
- The Architect's House
  All pictures by Tan Hock Beng
- Integral Education Centre
  All pictures by Tan Hock Beng
- Beijing Ju'er Hutong
  All pictures courtesy of Wu Liangyong
- Reuter House
  Pictures by Albert Lim and Tan Hock Beng
- Stage in the Forest
  Pictures courtesy of Kengo Kuma
- The Legian
  Pictures by Tan Hock Beng, Andra Matin and Dedi Kusnadi
- Wat Pa Sunanthawanaram
  All pictures courtesy of Architects 49 Ltd. Photos by Skyline Studio Ordinary Partnership
- Jayakody House
  All pictures by Tan Hock Beng
- Murasakino Wakuden
  All pictures courtesy of Waro Kishi. Photos by Hiroyuki Hirai
- Akeno Village Solar Bath Houses
  All pictures by Yoshio Kato
- 170 Bukit Timah Road
  All pictures courtesy of Kerry Hill. Photos by Albert Lim
- Bumi Asah
  All pictures by Tan Hock Beng
- The Serai
  All pictures courtesy of Kerry Hill
- Rimbun Dahlan
  All pictures courtesy of Hijas Kasturi
- House at Chatsworth Park
  Pictures by Benjamin Yu
- House at Blair Road
  All pictures courtesy of Richard Ho
- House at Everton Road
  Pictures by Albert Lim and Tan Hock Beng

ACKNOWLEDGEMENTS

Co-authoring and completing this book together has been an interesting experience. Commonalities and differences were brought together and argued at length. Several friends have also contributed their thoughts and offered valuable suggestions. Their experiences, insights and friendships have been a great inspiration. Their patience is also deeply appreciated.

But first, our thanks are due to our publisher, Lena Lim of Select Books, who has been intimately and passionately involved in every stage of the book, as well as Clara Pong for her ability to co-ordinate the whole project. Both Lena and Clara have also energetically and expertly kept the wheels turning when both authors displayed an inevitable tendency to stray outside the topics of discussion during every meeting.

Ko Hui Huy of Duet Design has once again done a marvellous job in the layout of the book. Her able assistant Chia Aik Beng also deserves special mention. In particular, we would also wish to record our sincere appreciation to the editor Nallamma Winslow for painstakingly and patiently combing through the text.

We are especially grateful to Charles Correa for his keen enthusiasm in the book and for kindly agreeing to write the Foreword. His trenchant writing has always been graced by a unique penetrative simplicity.

For reading and responding to various parts of the book, and for their honest opinions, we owe tremendous debts to many friends who have contributed in unchartable ways. They are all acknowledged below. We would also like to extend our particular gratitude to many others who have graciously shared their time and helped in sourcing materials as well as providing them. To all of them, our deep appreciation.

They are: C. Anjalendran, Geoffrey Bawa, Ernesto Bedmar, Bill Bensley, Lek Bunnag, Chua Beng Huat, Nondita Correa-Mehrotra, Channa Daswatte, Chanura Gunatilake, Hendra Hadiprana, Sindhu Hadiprana, Maria Hartati, Kerry Hill, Richard Ho Kong Fatt, Ho Kwoncjan, Kazuhiro Ishii, Sumet Jumsai, Hijas Kasturi, Yoshio Kato, Waro Kishi, Kengo Kuma, Dedi Kusnadi, Dharmali Kusumadi, Kwok Kian Woon, Cecilia Leong-Faulkner, Jimmy Lim, Prof Luo Xiao wei, Andra Matin, Mok Wei Wei, Khaisri Paksukcharern, Jeremy and Kate Penn, Robert Powell, Anura and Sundarika Ratnavibhushana, Nithi Sthapitanonda, Kevin Tan, Teh Joo Heng, Erwin J.S. Viray and Prof Wu Liangyong.

William S.W. Lim
Tan Hock Beng